True love;

Breaking the Cycle of Failed Relationships

By: Rhonda Fried BC,MS,RN

With Stanley Crossland II

Artwork by Katie Alyse Kravitz

This book is dedicated to the memory of Dr Robert N. Traisman, who saved my life when I was 16, by letting me sit in his office for a year, put my feet up on his desk and reading comics. He did this in exchange for convincing my parents it was a matter of life and death for them to let me support myself by moving into my own apartment. He was a smart one you see, because by tolerating that horrible behavior, one day I felt so bad that I decided it couldn't get any worse if I talked to him, so I finally put the comics down and started talking. Thus began my journey where through counseling the process of healing began in my life.

Years later, when I discovered the keys to helping myself, and others, find the path to self-love and a fulfilling life, I decided to write this book. I have seen one person after another read it, and when they apply the concepts and ideas contained within, wonderful changes start to occur in their lives. It is my sincere hope this book helps you find healing, balance and love in your life too!!!

Table of Contents

"Start by doing what's necessary; then do what's possible; and suddenly you are doing the impossible"

St Francis of Assisi

Introduction

How I came to write this book

I am about to share with you some secrets. Thirty years ago, like you, I would look at everyone around me and wonder what was wrong with me. Why did everyone else seem happy when I never was? Why did things come easily for other people? Why did everyone find it so easy to laugh and appear happy in love? Why were my love relationships always painful and, especially, why did it take me so long to get out of them knowing they were?

As with many of my colleagues in psychiatry, I was attracted to this field after healing some wounds and finding answers to many of those questions. Once I found them, I wanted to share them with others. Help them out of the deep and vast voids of depression, which often occur, along with other mental illnesses. Over the years, as a psychiatric clinical specialist at first and later as a psychiatric nurse practitioner, I have used the techniques learned during my years of study and adapted some of them to help many people solve problems. Professionally, I felt a strong sense of accomplishment, but there was one area in my life that continued to be a challenge.

Like many women, I was always attracted to the "wrong" man. Constantly in relationships where I ended up feeling lonely, unappreciated, tired and unloved. Always, I found myself in relationships where I was the one giving 100% effort, all the while getting close to nothing in return. When I needed help, no one was there to help me! However, when they needed me I was ready and willing to give help. I gave men 1st, 2nd, 3rd, 7th and 20th chances. I forgave and forgave and forgave! I paid their bills and hoped for a better future. I believed their excuses and lies, because being in a relationship was so much better than being alone.

Alone, the vast empty void! No one wants you. No one calls you. You are all alone, and you will always be alone. Everyone pities you and you fear they are secretly laughing at your lonely life. So empty, sad; starving for love and attention. Worst of all, true love never seems to come knocking. The pain is very real, physically palpable and nearly unbearable at times.

Certainly, it's better to be in a sick relationship with the hope of a "cure", than all alone and unwanted! Wasting away and shriveling up, with the whole world happily going on all around you, not seeming to notice you are even there. It's like you are invisible. It's like you don't matter at all. What is there to talk about? There is no drama, no love - you are so sad and so lonely that even you can't bear to think about it.

I remember what it's like to think it's so much better to keep going around the old merry go round. Go ahead, call him! It's ok, you're lonely, you need someone to hold and comfort you. And for a little while, hope returns. Did you see how happy he was to hear from you? Did he say thanks for giving him another chance? Did he promise this time would be different? Did you believe him?

I know this much, and you won't like it! He or she is the same person you met, with the same inability to commit to much less function in a healthy relationship, as he/she displayed the last time you gave it a try. He/she still has the same issues, the same addictions, the same selfish perspective and the same dysfunctional qualities that caused you to leave in the first place.

Guess what? Here is THE SECRET! Let me bring the cat out of the bag right away. I had to face this very same reality.

YOU will have to change if YOU want YOUR life to change.

I too had fantasies. Fantasies of a handsome husband, one I could depend on for love and financial support, with whom I could have children. We would live in a big beautiful house, in a big beautiful suburb and live happily ever after. I envisioned a beautiful wedding, with a gorgeous gown, tons of fresh flowers everywhere, the sun shining on us forever..... I had everything but the happiness and the sunshine. I had that wedding, and that was the end of the dream. What had I done wrong?

Alot of stormy weather had to pass before I found a more realistic, yet incredibly satisfying dream. The great news is the dream of a strong and loving relationship can indeed be had. I promise you that! Further, I promise you achieving it will be worth your effort if you fully commit to it. But, in order for any dream to become a reality, you have to work for it so that it can come to fruition. You have to change.

Are YOU willing to change who YOU are in order to get YOUR DREAMS?

Let me share with you a bit of my personal history. When I was young, I didn't think very highly of myself. I never had a relationship that lasted very long, mostly because I was too insecure and needy. I can think of two that pretty much illustrate my problems.

The first one happened while I was in nursing school. I had just graduated college with plans on becoming a psychologist when I started to analyze the number of years it would take to get my Ph.D. You see, at the time, in the late 70's, getting into a clinical psychology Ph.D. program was very, very difficult. I considered I might be better off getting a degree as a nurse, which would then allow me to work while continuing my education. The plan turned out to be a good course of action for me.

So, shortly after graduation, I enrolled in nursing school. I had been dating a "nice" boy who, despite having no formal education, had the same religion as myself, a good income, a nice car and his own condominium. He had taken over his father's business and was doing well. I had been seeing him for about a year.

One day, taking a break between classes, I called him. I can't tell you why I did, but something was nagging at me. I called him, and immediately his voice didn't sound right. I quickly got off the phone, jumped in my car (ditching a class) and went right to his condo. I began opening his door with my key, only to find him at the door with the chain on. It was pretty obvious what was going on, and I immediately melted into tears. To his credit, he didn't lie to me, but he did try to make excuses and asked if we could talk.

I put on my brave face and took a deep breath (by then I'd been in counseling for a while and had learned how to calm myself down). I pulled myself together and went downstairs to a restaurant to wait for him. I was, and still remain, proud I could even do that because inside I felt completely destroyed. And let's be honest, if I really knew what I was doing I should have just left without giving him any chance to talk. I had not yet developed the proper sense of self-respect necessary to refuse tolerating any of this.

But my expectations had come true. I knew I was unworthy. I knew I was unlovable. I could never count on anyone to be true to me or be honest with me, and it was always going to be just a matter of time until everything would fall apart again, leaving me alone once more. Unloved and unworthy of love, just like always!

Boyfriend number two, let's call him Sexy Man. Wherever we went, women threw themselves at him, often right in front of me. They would literally move between us and position themselves to block me. Funny thing is that wasn't even the worst part!

The worst part was that he had pictures of his old girlfriend, Sarah, around his apartment, causing him to lovingly and longingly speak of her. I wished I could be that "wonderful Sarah", even though he made it clear I could never be her in his mind, let alone replace her. I did everything I could to make myself more attractive. I ran 5 days a week, between 3 to 8 miles, and worked out lifting weights for an hour on most of those days too. I don't think I had an ounce of fat on me. Yet, to Sexy Man, I was still imperfect, still "fat". I was always "cute", but not "sexy".

The bottom line is I was trying to change who I was, losing whatever identity I did have to the all-encompassing endeavor of making me fit his definition of the perfect woman.

I dated him for two years before I realized: "Hey, I'm about to hit thirty. My biological clock is ticking!" At the time I had a lovely girlfriend that was involved with a man who had 'commitment issues'. She had been with him for five years. Did I want that? I knew enough to know I wanted to get married and I needed to do it soon if I were going to be able to have children. This logic gave me the necessary will to break up with number two and begin looking for someone who truly displayed 'husband material'.

As a footnote to the story and a kind of pleasant turn of events, about two years later I was working out at the health club where Sexy Man and I belonged when a woman approached me. Keep in mind that I was still friendly with Sexy Man and had spoken to him recently wherein he told me he was not seeing anyone. She said, "Hi, are you Rhonda?" I answered that I was. She introduced herself as Sexy Man's girlfriend of a year and a half (Poor girl)

She said she knew who I was because Sexy Man talked about me all the time, not to mention he had pictures of me all around his apartment. He had replaced his pictures of the glorious Sarah with pictures of me. How crazy is that? It was then I understood his way of avoiding commitment was to be magically and impossibly in love with whoever the last girlfriend was. I tried to do her a favor by telling her about all the Sarah pictures, politely as possible suggesting she consider moving on. I never talked to either of them again after that, but do you think she listened?

We like to fantasize we will be the one to break the mold; he will love us enough to change. If we are good enough, beautiful enough, thin enough or 'something enough' - it will all work out. Sadly that type of thinking never works out in the long run.

Shortly after hitting 30, I was engaged. It never occurred to me to question why he was in such a hurry to be engaged after dating only two months. I have no idea how my family pulled together such a beautiful lavish wedding 6 months after I met him! I had the wedding of my dreams! That was the last good day of our marriage.

The morning after, we missed the plane for our honeymoon. I was inconsolable and he was angry. On day two we finally made it to paradise, then promptly had the biggest blowup fight ever! Who was this man? He was a stranger, of course. He was nothing like the person he portrayed himself to be for the last 6 months. It was all a big act, and now I understood what the hurry was about. If we had dated longer, I was sure to find out that the whole relationship was based on lies and deception. I quickly realized I made a terrible mistake marrying him and started to think about how could I get out of this mistake?

The next flight out wasn't for 24 hours, and by then, he had convinced me it was just the stress of the last day, that he wasn't really the controlling, frightening, abusive, screaming man I had just witnessed; and to give him another chance. I of course did! Truth be told, there were other reasons I decided to stay. I felt horribly embarrassed about my parents spending all that money, I thought about the work of returning all those gifts to their senders and how embarrassed I would be that I had been so incredibly stupid. I made a promise to myself to wait six months, and then leave him.

It took about another six months for the next meltdown. After which began what I like to call now 'the seduction of the abuser'. Periods of loving attention, promises of change, all kinds of reassurances that it won't happen again. This would cause me to think – no it sure won't! But then his crying, begging and pestering each time I tried to leave, his promises and his seeming remorse would make me pause. I would say to myself "I'm over 30. I want to have children. Maybe I could just have a child or two and then divorce him. I'll bide my time."

I never meant to marry an abuser. That was the one type of man I promised myself I would not tolerate. When I dated, I asked him about his style of dealing with conflicts. I told him "I can't tolerate confrontation, yelling or bad temper." I shared with him how my father yelled at me all the time, how he was always angry when I was young. I said "You have to understand that's the one thing I can't deal with!" He assured me he never yelled and absolutely never lost his temper. The pattern I call the "seduction of the abuser" goes in cycles. After a meltdown, there is a honeymoon period where it becomes easy to convince yourself that the behavior was an aberration....until it happens again. In my case, it went on for nine miserable years.

But how did I let myself get there to begin with? And why did I stay so long? Why was it so hard for me to leave? Why was the fear of being alone so paralyzing for so long?

The answers are much clearer in hindsight. I am very lucky I got connected with a terrific therapist. Even more influential might have been the discovery of Cognitive Behavioral Therapy while reading the book "_Feeling Good_" by _Dr. Burns_ in college! As well as a gift from my sister, _Louise Hay's_ "_You Can Heal Your Life_", which essentially uses the same principles, while I was going through my divorce. Both these books opened a whole new world to me as a professional and as a person.

Eventually I came up with a plan. I looked at elements of people whose lives were successful. I read a number of memoirs on people who were happy and in healthy relationships, slowly realizing I too was as entitled to those as much as anyone else. I began hunting for the qualities that made for good partnerships. In general, my research showed the most successful partnerships occur when each person comes to the relationship feeling whole, with something to give, the partnership varying as to when one took care of the other.

That was when the logic hit me. It is impossible to "rescue" or "fix" someone, the fantasy being he/she will later love you and appreciate you and take care of you. It just never works that way! When you rescue someone, or try to fix him/her, you only end up angry with him/her because it doesn't work. The old adage, one I have witnessed a thousand times as a professional, will forever be true: Only the person needing fixing can fix themselves!

And until they are whole, until they address their own issues head on, they can't be in a healthy relationship. So this can never be the way a good relationship starts. What you will have when you choose someone who needs fixing is a one-sided relationship where you do all the giving and you end up feeling lonely, unloved, underappreciated and unfulfilled.

Do you want to know where to find the loneliest people on earth? You will find them in a one-sided relationship. There is nothing sadder than being with someone you know will never be able to love you the way you need to be loved. There are many, many women who stay in these kinds of relationships. They are convinced that no one else will want them at all. They stay with abusers and liars and cheaters because they think it's better than being alone. They settle for predictable misery, while dreaming the ultimate fantasy: something will magically change!

I am telling you, as someone who had to change herself, as a professional who has seen others change – the person who has to change is YOU!

You have to face the fear of failure to find success. You have to rid your life of the negative patterns and traits you developed before there is a space for something better. You have to examine and change some of your assumptions, and work to improve them in order to improve your life. You have the power to do this, and I will explain how.

Personally, the first step was to face my fear of being alone. Not only that, I had to believe it was something I could survive. I decided to embrace the idea that the loneliness of being in an unhealthy relationship, the anger and frustration I felt, the effect it had on my health (obesity and irritability) and the health of my child, was worse than my fear of being alone.

I began using positive mental imagery and affirmations about my future. I started to envision what a healthy partner would be like. One who could take care of me as well as let me take care of him. I imagined what a mentally healthy partner would act like, along with how I might recognize those qualities. I tried to visualize someone who would be kind, patient and warm. I still had the desire for more children so I imagined him as having children, loving them and accepting mine as his own.

I imagined him as sensitive enough to share a conversation about our feelings and caring enough to respond when I was upset about something. Vaguely I thought about what physical features I was attracted to, but I realized I felt more strongly about the warmth the person exuded. I fantasized about what kind of character he would have and what some of his values would be. I used affirmations to convince myself that it was possible to obtain this kind of relationship. Then a miraculous thing happened.

Within a very short period of time after I did these things I found him, and I knew within the first hour. But to be sure, I took my time and we let the relationship develop slowly. I write this book after having been married for sixteen wonderful years.

I decided to write this book because I know if I was able to do this for myself, then surely I can help others obtain the same goal.

A few years ago I worked with a client named Brian who was distraught after breaking up with a woman he had dated for years. After some time into the relationship she was ready for a commitment, but he had already married and divorced twice in his life. He had broken up with her 6 months earlier, yet couldn't stop thinking about her and was having trouble moving on in his life.

By addressing his goals and fears in therapy, using the principles I am about to share with you, he realized he had nothing to lose by giving her a call and asking for another chance. Six months later they were happily married.

Joe and Patrick were two other men I worked with who had somewhat similar situations. Both felt they were with women they wanted to spend the rest of their life with, and both felt this commitment wasn't a step they could take until their life was set-up in a certain way. Men, in particular, feel a need to be established in a career and financially stable before they can make commitments in their life. By using the principles in the book, we clarified their goals and both realized that there was nothing to keep them from popping the question. The women in these relationships loved them for who they were, irrespective of their current financial standing, and both of them realized the ladies didn't want to be strung along for years with someone who was afraid of commitment.

The good news is together we identified their goals AND their partners' goals to come up with a simple solution: propose and get engaged. In both of these situations the women had absolutely no interest in ending the relationship once they knew the men were as serious as they were. Once there was a promise and a ring, both were happy, and two relationships that almost ended because of seemingly disparate goals were successfully salvaged.

For those of you with more analytical minds, it might help to know that all of the techniques described in this book are based on the science of the human mind. Many books have been written, with corresponding clinical studies done, about how the process of cognitive behavioral therapy (CBT) works to improve not only depression, but many other issues. CBT is essentially a way of reprogramming your brain to think differently! It requires a conscious monitoring of your thoughts to change them.

As mentioned previously, in the 1980's Dr. David Burns came out with the first book popularizing the theory and sharing the processes with the public. Originally developed in the 1960s by Dr Aaron Beck, CBT built on the theory and practice of Dr. Albert Ellis' _Rational Emotive Therapy_. The concepts espoused in CBT were big breakthroughs in the field of psychiatry because it proved that people could learn to think differently. It showed that a lot of the chronic, negative and fearful thoughts people perpetuate in their minds interfere with their ability to live healthy and happy lives.

These therapies recognized most people's behavior and emotions are based on their thoughts, yet it is also possible for people's thoughts to be changed and, when that happened, their lives changed!

The simplest example of how this works is when you go to a movie. The content of the movie will occupy your thoughts while watching it and often for several hours afterwards. While you are watching a happy movie and laughing, you feel good. If you are seeing a scary movie, you feel afraid. If you are watching a sad story, you might feel sad. The content of what is entered in our thoughts is what is real for us at that moment.

When we're not paying attention, all kinds of thoughts are running their own movie in our minds, affecting how we think and how we behave. Sometimes this movie is very dysfunctional and needs to be re-edited, maybe even rewritten. Once again the good news is the way we feel can be altered with some conscious work, practice and effort. We can change, or reprogram if you will, our dysfunctional/illogical thinking!

My intention in writing this book is to share with you the tools that helped me to a full recovery after a 25-year history of sick relationships. I worked my way into a very healthy, satisfying marriage with a wonderful, trustworthy partner. There are tools I used and techniques I adapted, or 'tweaked', to fit my personality. Throughout my career I have helped a number of clients apply these principles and end destructive relationships, moving on to find happy ones. All the steps discussed herein are based on the science of Cognitive Behavioral Therapy. Anyone can learn these steps, and more importantly, how to apply them to your own life. I promise they will help you nurture a healthier and happier life.

Author's note: As you read this book please remember that some of what you read will apply to you, and some will not. Use what works for you.

one

The Process of Finding Healthy Love

There are a lot of books and interesting history detailing how it is possible to teach yourself to think differently in order to find success in your life. From the late 1800s when the Nobel Laureate Dr. Ivan Pavlov developed his Behavioral Modification conditioning in dog studies, the ideas that behavior can be taught and nurtured influenced both psychology and popular culture.

Pavlov's studies began to be applied to humans in many areas of psychology, from Dr. Rollo May in the early 1900s, when he applied them to his Existential Therapy techniques, to the 1930s studies and writings on Rational Emotive Therapy by Dr. Albert Ellis, through to BF Skinner's Behavioral Modification Techniques. In looking at popular culture, especially in the professional sales field, starting in the 1930s' with Dale Carnegie's *How to Win Friends and Influence People* up to the 1950s' when Norman Vincent Peal published *"The Power of Positive Thinking"*, studies have been applied to human behavior teaching people you can harness your thoughts to achieve success in business and life. The outcome of having positive thoughts is feeling confident in who you are and what you are doing. The work that goes into being prepared, grounded and sure-footed produces positive results. One such example is how people's responses to you can be changed based on how you interact with them, and this is something that can be taught.

In the 1960s, Dr. Aaron Beck's "*Cognitive Behavioral Therapy*" integrated all this previous knowledge into a comprehensive and relatable set of techniques that became the basis for most psychotherapy today. Again, what makes his work so fantastic is it can be self-taught. This collective body of knowledge and techniques became the reigning standard, still utilized today as the quickest, most outcome effective approach to helping people change their emotions and behavior.

Many of the current self-help books on the market today which focus on teaching you how to become successful use or rely heavily on the knowledge and processes from these scientists studies and theories on human behavior. This book is also based on many of those principles too!

If you believed that just thinking differently would totally change your life for the better, what would stop you from pursuing your goals? Have you ever wondered how two people who were brought up in the same dysfunctional family can turn out so different? How one can be very successful and the other one repeats the same mistakes over and over again, much in the same way the parents did? The answer is that one of them has made a conscious decision not to follow in their family's footsteps, and that conscious decision affects their thinking and actions, so they avoid certain situations or behaviors that could interfere with their goals of having a very different kind of life.

We will talk about this more and I know you have heard this before, BUT OUR CHOICES, and the motivations behind them, ARE SO INFLUENTIAL TO THE LIFE WE HAVE!

In reading some of the books on finding success such as those already discussed or even ones like Steven Covey's "*The 7 Habits of Highly Effective*

People", one of the traits successful people have in common is a clear picture of their goal. They begin with 'an end in mind'. Also, they make a commitment to achieving their goal! One of the single best ways they do this is by using visualization to see it before it becomes a reality.

Once you have a clear picture of what you want to achieve, your daily choices become much easier. Does a choice get you closer or farther from your goal? Most successful people have a clear picture of what they want to achieve, and they aren't influenced by others who tell them they can't. No matter what happens, they refuse to quit. Over time they have learned to cultivate this positive attitude and believe the goal is their destiny - they WILL find a way! They have determination and perseverance. They have purpose.

Two of the most effective techniques for helping you achieve your goals are Visualizations and Affirmations. Visualizations help your brain feel comfortable and develop a picture of yourself meeting your goal, a process that positively affects your day-to-day decisions. Affirmations support visualizations in that they help remind you to believe in yourself, to feel confident you will be able to meet your goals.

What might surprise you is the science behind these techniques has been tested and studied, with the overwhelming conclusion brain training does indeed change the brain. A specific kind of test called a Spect Scan can show the parts of the brain that are engaged during different kinds of activities. We can actually learn to change how our brain works! Biofeedback is another measuring tool that shows us through practice our brain changes.

You see our brain doesn't recognize the difference between real and imagined practice. Consequently, if you continue to imagine negative outcomes for your relationships, you will act in ways that supports and often ultimately brings these outcomes to manifestation in your life. Conversely, on the positive side, you can practice training your brain to expect positive outcomes, and the more you do so, the more likely you will behave in a way that supports this, bringing to fruition these very sought after positive experiences for you.

When I first read about the inability of the brain to differentiate between real practice and imagined practice, I started using both visualization and affirmation techniques to better my performance as a nursing instructor. I started running through lectures in my head rather than using notes. I kept telling myself I knew my subject and didn't need to worry about all that I had learned somehow disappearing when it was time to speak. Instead of writing out the entire class lecture and reading verbatim from my notes, I wrote down the main topics to cover. I would practice in my mind the process of relating my points tied to each main topic, and if I found I missed anything important I meant to cover, I would add one reminder word about that to my notes.

Instead of pages of script, I ended up with one or two note cards. Also, I realized it would be more impactful for students to learn the major points, limiting the amount of points I wanted to convey so they would walk away from the lesson clear on the important topics. I improved my public speaking skills, and the positive feedback about my teaching really made me feel good about my job.

In spite of that, I quit teaching. Out of 100 students, I would obsess about the 3 that invariably wrote critical things about my approach, letting that upset me and drive me crazy. At that point in my life, despite all my studies and experiences, I was still practicing negative thinking that further supported my negative views of myself.

Many of my favorite self-help books have versions of these two techniques as their basis or main theme. "_The Secret_" by Rhonda Byrne is about the importance and need to set a crystal clear goal in order for it to happen.

In Louise Hays' "_You Can Heal Your Life_", she advocates using distinct visualizations along with powerful affirmations to release issues such as anger, hurt or regret that no longer serve your life.

One of my favorite writers is Augusten Burroughs! Augusten survived a bitterly painful childhood, finding a way to heal and cope, using humor to write about it. Laughter is wonderful medicine. In his book "_Possible Side Effects_" he tells the story of a friend, Christy, who was lamenting her inability to find a romantic partner.

Augusten, during many of his drunken binges, entertained himself by writing elaborate "personal ads" that he would often forget placing when he woke the next day. He was really kidding when he advised Christy to write down all the attributes she was looking for and place an ad, but she actually did it and was extremely specific when she did. She wrote a 10-page ad, in addition to paying for a full-page ad in a major New York newspaper. When Augusten realized she had actually done it, he was horrified, but since it was done at his suggestion he went along, helping her go through the replies. Both of them were afraid she would get none. However, soon enough they started to come, and she sorted them into a 'yes' pile and a 'no' pile.

One of the women she put into a "no" pile was a woman that Augusten felt 'looked right' for Christy. Initially, she dismissed this woman because of her hair color. So she went out with all the women in the 'yes' pile, including some that Augusten definitely saw red flags about, and continued to struggle to find the 'right' partner. Eventually she finished seeing all the women in her 'yes' pile, with no successful match, and they were talking about what to do next. Augusten remembered the red headed woman he thought would be right for her and encouraged Christy to go out with her, even though she didn't like red heads.

Months later, this woman ended up being the woman of Christy's dreams. Much of the time, the solution to happiness or unhappiness is right in front of us, and sometimes it takes an outsider to help us see that the answer is right there. Without realizing it, this woman did most of the steps this book will teach you how to do. This woman set a goal, clarified what she wanted, worked for the goal and eventually found it, just like I did 20 years ago.

The process is to clearly identify your goals, then take the steps to implement them. How many times have you heard this? More importantly, how many times have you actually followed the steps necessary to achieve these goals? Obviously, there are many aspects of implementation that can be very hard; it's a lot like embarking on a new exercise program or diet. The beginning is the hardest part, yet with practice many of these steps will become second nature.

In the studies regarding development of habits, it requires about 6 weeks to form a new habit. In the beginning, you have to push yourself to take the steps. You have to give yourself pep talks and remind yourself of the goal you are working to obtain. Gradually over the course of time, you have to fight with yourself less and less. Eventually, you wake up and do that run or walk your dogs or get to your trainer. The hardest part is always taking the first steps!

As you proceed through the steps in this book, each chapter will have a series of exercises designed to increase the likelihood of meeting your goals using tools that help you see a happier future. These exercises will fall into the categories of visualizations and affirmations. They will help you nurture, cultivate and develop the positive outlook necessary for you to achieve your goals. The clearer and more positive you become in the process the more likely you are to have success. Simple cause and effect! They may feel awkward at first, but practice them diligently and you will see wonderful results. Hopefully, as we move forward you will create some of your own visualizations and affirmations to aide in your personal journey.

Visualization One: *Comfort Place*

Close your eyes and create a wonderful space in your mind where you feel comfortable. Imagine this location in as much detail as possible. Imagine what to you is the perfect temperature. Imagine a place where you feel protected and very, very safe. Imagine the most comfortable chair or bed or couch, exactly the right amount of firmness and support, pillows and blankets, and decorate this place exactly the way you would if money and access were no object.

Now imagine relaxing in this place, feeling totally safe and comfortable. Pay attention to your heart as the beat slows, your breath as it softens and just enjoy how being here feels. Know that this is a place you can come to at any time to feel comfortable and safe......

Stay here for at least 15 minutes.

Affirmation for Safety and Comfort:

"I am comfortable and safe here in my special place."

Step One: Define your Partner and Your Goal

The first step is to imagine your goal, keeping in mind you need to be as specific as possible. It can't just be a vague dream, a movie star image, a happily ever after fantasy. Appearances are important. Most likely, that has probably been the driving force behind those you've connected with so far. We can't change our instincts. We will be more attracted to some than to others. So why is it then that the men you are attracted to often result in being the worst one's for you? Why are you always attracted to men who break your heart, abuse you emotionally, are unemployed/underemployed or are unreliable and unfaithful?

There is a buffet of reasons we are attracted to unhealthy relationships. That being said, we actually don't need to understand all of them to change our destructive behavior patterns or to learn how to make healthier choices. If you are choosing one bad relationship after another, can we now both agree your process or logic is flawed, and there is probably a reason? Some unidentified issue has unconsciously attracted you to the same guy in different packages.

Every time you see an advertisement on tv about food, you don't get up and eat, do you? Every time you pass a pizza or ice cream shop, you don't stop. Every time a driver cuts you off you may think of rear ending them or worse, but you don't. Thinking something doesn't mean you have to act on it. So having established that every day you think things but don't act on them, why have you permitted yourself to act on your urge to continue in relationships you know to be unhealthy?

The difference is that in one area of your life, perhaps driving, or eating or at work with a rude boss or obnoxious co-workers, you have already built in your internal response to yes or no. You think before you act. Somehow in your love life, you've neglected to think first. As a result, acting without thinking first has become a habit.

The way to break this pattern and change is to become more conscious of your thoughts and decisions. You need learn to identify the issue before you feel completely sucked into a bad relationship and out spin out of control. And because you will still be in control you will end it before it goes too far or gets too messy. The process of identifying your unconscious drive will help you recognize and discern more clearly what/who is truly good for you and what/who is not.

Next, let's identify your goals for a good relationship. Are you looking for a companion? A spouse? Fidelity? A man to father your child? Think of this as a very specific job opening and write your ad. No one will see this but you. List as many physical and emotional characteristics as possible, in addition to social and occupational ones. Is a job a necessity? How about living out of town, away from either your or his relatives? Do you want financial security or just emotional security, or both? Is health or diet an issue? Are smoking or drinking, and their subsequent attitude towards them, important? Are children an issue?

Think of the major source of conflicts in relationships and define your needs as far as money, family and sex. What would make you happy and what would make you comfortable. Can you close your eyes and imagine what this would feel like? Spend some time, as much as possible, just asking yourself what you want and what you really need? See what images come to mind and write them down as they come. Like every other exercise in this book, expect that this will initially be more difficult than it sounds; actually trying to see this person and this person's qualities.

Maybe you can just imagine what being with this person would feel like. Write down these images. It would be helpful to buy a binder to keep this list in, even laminating/decorating it because you will be referring back to it many times. This list is very important! Look it over numerous times, adding whatever comes to mind and giving yourself plenty of time to complete or amend it. You might even completely re-do your list when a situation causes you to realize your needs and opinions have changed as you go through the process.

Now begin to go through it again and rate the characteristics as either
1.) Non-negotiable and Very Important.
2.) Important
3.) Nice But Not Essential

Congratulations! You have now finished the first step. Be proud you are taking the time to clarify who and what you now want in your life from this day forward. Start to believe this list will indeed manifest itself. Begin to encourage yourself that you too can have the life you always dreamed of.

Visualization Two: *You with your partner*

Imagine yourself in that safe and comfortable place you created before. It is warm and cozy and beautiful all at the same time. You are relaxed, sitting in your favorite place, your heartbeat is slow and your breathing is soft and deep. You can even count while you are breathing, and it seems to take almost an infinite period of time to breathe in and breathe out, because you feel like you are floating.

Now, once you have re-created that comfortable place, imagine you are there with a very close friend whom you love. You don't need to see the person as much as feel what it would be like to be with someone you love, who supports you and loves you back. Imagine what it feels like to be in the wonderful comfort of your favorite place with someone who loves you as much as you love them. Feel the sensations occurring inside and outside, how this person warms you when you're with them. Savor this feeling. Pay attention and remember what this feels like.

Affirmation for love:

"I am completely comfortable and safe in my relationship. I feel safe to love, because I am accepted and appreciated in my relationship. I have felt the warm embrace of love and I will feel it again."

Step Two: Becoming worthy and establishing your personal goal list.

You are beginning to imagine yourself happy and content with your future partner. Close your eyes again and see what you look like. How are you feeling? How do you feel about yourself? What about you would you change in order to feel better about yourself? Write these things down. These are long-term goals.

Many of us are convinced that we're not worthy of being loved unless we look a certain way. Many of us are convinced that we are too broken to deserve love. We look at magazines and TV and make incorrect conclusions as to perfection. YOU ARE WORTHY OF LOVE BECAUSE EVERY ONE OF US IS WORTHY OF LOVE!

If you have a very hard time believing that then you will need to spend time in working on your negative thinking. Maybe try an exercise I have many of my clients go through: spend time on the bus or in another public place looking around the crowd for people who seem content. Do they appear exceptional in some way? Are they all perfect looking? Do they all look successful? Or do they seem to be average people, like you?

Most of us have a few traits we would like to change about ourselves, and/or patterns of behavior that determine the way we are living. It is helpful to know that how we think and behave is learned, and we can retrain both our thinking and our behavior. Nothing is permanent if we don't want it to be!

When you imagine yourself happy, if you see yourself in a way that is very different in appearance than what you see now, you need to write down what the differences are. Identify what is missing or askew. This list is your personal goal list. It is not necessary to accomplish these goals to obtain your future partner. But it is very helpful for your self-esteem to start listening to the words you tell yourself each day.

If you tell yourself each day as you eat a piece of chocolate cake that you will diet tomorrow, and tomorrow never comes, you need to stop telling yourself you will diet. If you are staying up on the internet every night when you know you should be sleeping, thus dragging yourself half-awake through each day, then the problem you have is not with time, but credibility with yourself! This has a terrible impact on your self-esteem.

It is very important to like yourself and feel worthy of being loved. The easiest step in this direction is to break the pattern of making 'tomorrow promises' that aren't kept and start establishing small goals achievable today. Every long-term goal consists of taking several small, incremental steps to get there. While a common problem in not meeting a personal goal is making promises for tomorrow, an equally debilitating commonality is not truly understanding the process of making changes in your life. REAL LONG-TERM GOALS ARE ONLY ACCOMPLISHED BY TAKING THE TIME TO BREAK THEM DOWN INTO SMALL, ATTAINABLE GOALS that can be done in the present.

Try to pick something simple and easy you would like to change in your life. For example, most of us wish we would exercise more. Typically, the goal I have heard is go to the gym three times a week for one hour. Many times it is the goal that has to first be modified because an attainable goal has to be one you can take a step towards as immediately as possible!

The reason for this is that we are too good at making empty promises daily to ourselves. Commonly, we make the very same false promises every day. When you make these false promises and then don't keep them, it negatively affects your self-esteem because you don't believe yourself. It is like you are sabotaging your own credit score with yourself. This whole process will be impossible unless you have the necessary trust and belief in yourself to accomplish your goals.

If your own words to yourself are meaningless, nothing will ever change in your life. You must learn how to trust yourself, believe yourself and prove yourself reliable to you! This can be done daily by performing small mental exercises to instill confidence that you mean what you say. If you don't believe you, how can you expect anyone else to take you seriously?

Real personal change takes place by setting a goal and breaking it down into attainable steps. Each step should be small enough that you could take action to make it happen as soon as possible. Every time you keep your word to yourself by completing one of these small steps, your self-esteem and confidence will grow.

When you begin to practice this kind of mental exercise every day you begin to both believe yourself and in yourself, and that is how you become a person another person would want to be around. If you don't like yourself, then when you do find the right partner, you will do everything you can to sabotage the relationship because you won't believe you deserve this wonderful relationship in your life (sounds familiar?). Your own feelings of unworthiness will eat away at your psyche.

As mentioned before, this book incorporates the techniques of Cognitive Behavioral Therapy to change your life and your unhealthy thinking. I can assure you perfection is not necessary to be worthy of love. As long as you work on improving your life, you will find things will begin to change.

If you know you are taking steps to feel better about yourself, these steps will serve as support in your efforts to find a more suitable partner. We are always in process and always changing. Your life is a working canvas; you need to create the environment that allows this miracle of finding a partner to happen by believing in yourself and your worth.

Do you see what the first step is about? Not changing your relationships with others, but changing your relationship with yourself. THE

VERY FIRST RELATIONSHIP THAT OFTEN NEEDS TO BE FIXED IS THE ONE YOU HAVE WITH YOU!

Let me share an example of this from my life. As a nurse, I never believed I was a creative person. I couldn't fathom the idea of producing artwork of any kind. For a period of time, I worked as a visiting nurse in people's homes. In one particular home, I walked in and was transfixed by the décor, there was vivid, rich handmade works of needlepoint. Paintings hung all over the walls that were warm and inviting. There were lush, deep yellow sunflowers painted on many of the surfaces that really caught my attention. When I commented on how lovely they were the patient said her daughter had come in from out of town to help her recover from her illness and had created the paintings. Immediately, I asked the daughter if I could purchase one of the paintings or have her do a similar design in my home on some of the decor. The conversation went something like this:

Her: "Yes, I can paint some things for you, but how would you like it if I taught you how to do this yourself."
Me: "No, you don't know me, I don't have an artistic bone in my body. I can't do that."
Her: "I really can teach you how to do this, so you can decorate whatever you want, whenever you want, however you want."
Me: "You don't understand, I can't do anything artistic."
Her: "Do you wish you could?"
Me: "Yes, of course I wish I could!"
Her: "Would you like to be able to paint this?"
Me: "Absolutely."
Her: "Well, if you truly want to, then you can. If you sincerely want to learn how to do this, I promise that I can teach you how."
Me: "Really, well, I'm very busy with work and my child. How long would this take? I don't have much free time to devote hours to learning a new skill."

Her: "I can teach you to paint this sunflower in 2 hours."
Me: (With a look of disbelief) "Ok! Let's try."

And with that a whole new world opened up to me. Now, when people come into my home they find all kinds of artwork that I have created, from a pattern of ivy around the living room walls, to beautiful hand thrown celadon porcelain carved vases. I went from thinking I had no artistic abilities whatsoever to becoming an artist.

In other words, the only thing stopping me from becoming an artist was my belief that it was a FACT I couldn't. This woman broke down the long held notion existing in my brain by presenting me with a very small, attainable step with which I couldn't argue. She gave me the gift of opening a whole new world of creativity I had long forgotten was there by presenting a small enough first step that allowed me to see it was possible. I honestly doubt it would have ever happened if she had presented me with some type of huge project.

Lets take that concept and apply it to one of your own personal goals.

Consider the aforementioned exercise goal: what would it look like if you broke it down into attainable steps you can take action on today?

Personal Goal: Go to the gym three times a week
Realistic Thought Process: Increase your exercise level just a bit
Possible Action Steps: Take the stairs today once instead of the elevator; park at the farthest corner of the parking lot at work; walk to the corner of the block to take your cigarette break; stroll halfway down the block when you go out to get the mail

Writing this book has been a personal goal for a long time. I have thought about writing it for fifteen years, the very same fifteen years since I created and utilized this program for myself, which helped bring about the relationship of my dreams in every way. Since then, I have counseled many men and women using this same process, watching one after another achieve their personal and professional goals. Each time I've done this, I've taken a few minutes to write down the ideas, processes and techniques that worked, modifying the outline over and over again. Suddenly, three essential situations changed in my life to create the space for me to accomplish my goal.

First, the community mental health agency where I worked was going out of business. As a bit of a tangent, I would like to share that the people who elect to work in this field are a very noble group, committed not only to helping those with psychiatric issues, but helping those who have absolutely few or no resources of their own. They are often homeless, jobless, and penniless; involved in chaotic relationships along with often being in severe emotional pain. The many personal stories I have witnessed of what humans do to other humans are heartbreaking! It takes a special person to do this day after day, year after year, when much easier work could be chosen than this, and I was honored to work with some fantastic, dedicated physicians and therapists.

That being said, when the community center closed each of us had to make a decision about where we would work. Every single colleague except me elected to continue working in the same type of community mental health agency. I made a personal decision to make a move towards a private practice. It was a difficult and frightening decision, both personally and professionally.

The one time I had worked in private practice before had not worked out well. I saw clients subjected to expensive services they didn't all really need, and along with that, had other ethical concerns and philosophical differences of opinion.

Despite my concerns I joined a private practice group. It turned out to be a wonderful decision. No, a gift! Instead of the extreme mental fatigue brought on by dealing with crisis after crisis all day long, I often had nice, manageable days. I enjoyed my job and the people I worked with, along with the environment I worked in. Now, during my time off, I finally had the mental energy left to finally write my book on my time off, instead of recuperating between crises.

The second serendipitous situation was shortly after I began writing one of my friends sold his business. He told me he was looking to get back into copywriting, something he had done before his last venture. When I asked him about his experience in writing and publishing, he shared that he had done some freelance editing before and agreed to help me with the project. Suddenly I had even more motivation to get this done. I had an experienced writer to help guide my idea to fruition.

Finally, after I began writing I shared with a colleague what I was doing and her immediate response was "hurry up and finish, I need to read that book!" Wow! There it was - a person who said they needed to hear what I had to say because they too yearned for answers. What could be more motivating than knowing you already have an audience?

Let me point out here there is one more element, which was imperative to not only developing my own clientele base, but my ability to sit down and begin working on this project: over the years I had built up credibility with myself through the processes I had been using. My own belief that I could accomplish what I set out to do, one small step at a time, had been cemented as FACT in my own mind.

Long ago I had already established the goal of writing this book in my mind. As I wrote the introduction, the visualization of completing it after all these years further increased my confidence. As I completed each page, I was reinforcing my vision that this would actually happen and no longer remain just a fantasy. As I finished each section I felt an enormous sense of satisfaction, accomplishment and pride that I had taken one step at a time to do what I had promised myself I would. My friend and my colleague increased my motivation to get it done now through their encouragement. Success leads to more success, and here you are reading the final version of my dream.

Voila! The end result ends up reinforcing the process used to reach the goal!

All three of these fortuitous events also created the mental space and motivation for me to meet my goal. Creating space in your life for good things to happen is the next step you will need to take for your dreams to become reality. We will discuss how to go about doing this in the next section.

Visualization for Goal Attainment:

Think about a goal you have decided to work on in your life. In my case, I imagined a completed and published book that people would find helpful, and now you are reading it. If your goal is to exercise more, imagine yourself physically fit, toned and strong. If it is a work promotion, imagine yourself at the next level, performing the tasks and work required of that position. Whatever it is, imagine yourself performing the actions and tasks necessary to achieve that goal.

How do you feel about reaching your goal? How have you changed? Are you proud? Are you credible with yourself? Are you happy? Imagine yourself enjoying success. Believe you can do it!

Affirmation for Success:

"I am happy and grateful today. Life has provided me the skills, opportunity, drive, credibility and determination to be successful in my chosen path."

Step Three: Clearing the Deck

The next step is making space for this new relationship to come into your life. There is a concept in physics wherein mass will shift to level off into a vacant space. We can apply this same law to our own mind space. No one new can enter your life if you're too busy to allow for this happen. If you meet the most perfect person in the world but aren't free to see them a second time until a month after the first date, it won't ever happen. There has to be a space for them to enter your life.

They have to feel they will be as important to you as you want to be to them. If you don't make it a priority to provide room in your life, then a relationship won't happen. If you are occupying your time rescuing your girlfriend, answering drunken booty calls or saving homeless cats it won't happen. If you are too preoccupied with your career, it won't happen. If you aren't willing to make this important, it won't happen. Mentally, you have to do some housecleaning and get rid of the clutter.

You have to deny the booty call and erase all those phone numbers, or at least block them. You can't be traveling out of town every weekend and expect to have time to develop a relationship. You can do those things and have fun, or you can do lots of other things to keep yourself busy, but knowing humans are very fragile and tender beings it doesn't take a lot to scare people off. If you have come to the point where you say "I want a partner and it's important to me", you will have to put this intention into motion by creating the space, time and attention necessary to make this happen.

When you identify a potential mate, you need to have the time set aside to spend with them in order to determine if you want this person to stay. I see enough attractive and interesting people in my office to know that there are plenty of good people around. The problem with the clutter of living is that it often does two things: First, it creates camouflage so that you can't be seen. Second, it keeps you from being able to see others.

It amazes me how many people think they can keep on doing the same thing day after day while hoping for something miraculous to change their lives. I suppose a great example is the lottery ticket buyer. One person buys the ticket and dreams wistfully, yet by buying the ticket they at least have a chance in winning. The other person laughs at the ticket buyer and never buys a ticket. You can't win if you don't play!

One piece of clutter to eliminate is the 'convenient relationship/booty call person' that you know is a "relationship" going nowhere. If you are absolutely positive that it will go nowhere, you must find the courage to end it now. Your time and energy are very valuable. There is a very real possibility the partner you seek is someone you already know and never thought of in that way. Clutter clouds both the mind and your vision. You have to stop, look up and look around. YOU HAVE TO CHANGE FOR YOUR LIFE TO CHANGE!

I often ask clients to think for a minute about people they come across every day, especially those who might seem particularly friendly or thoughtful. These could be people you pass every day on the elevator, at work, at school or on the bus. If instead of the half-awake preoccupied way we often live life, what if you were to instead look around and imagine if anyone you see could be a possible partner, then it becomes very real that this could happen. If you then look at this person with that goal in mind, you might begin to treat them differently, act differently and subsequently open space in your life. When you are free of superficial drama you might be surprised as to how much more approachable you become.

Clifton was a young man with which I had this conversation. He wasted no time answering he usually took the same bus to work each day where he saw a young woman who would smile at him every morning. They would look at each other, say hello, and he'd sit in his usual seat a few rows away from where she usually sat. I asked "What would happen if either of them moved, or if instead one day he took the chance to sit next to her?" It had never occurred to him, and sadly, I don't think he ever did. He was too afraid.

You have to overcome your inhibitions about hurting people and being polite if you want to find what you want. You can easily waste a whole lifetime being polite, but alone. Wasting someone's time and energy in an unhealthy relationship, or letting them waste yours, is unfair to you both. If you have been hanging around with someone for years because they are there and you are afraid of being alone, I realize it will be frightening to make a change and release them. But if the worst case scenario were to occur and months or years later you find yourself watching film noir with a bottle of wine for one, I doubt they will turn you down if you want to go back to your old ways.

Millions of people live unfulfilling lives consumed with unhealthy activities like this, and trust me - you will have no problem finding someone else to indulge you in the future should you decide it's better to be in a bad relationship than be alone. Professionally, I have seen many clients spend too much time being with someone they don't care about, and whom they know really doesn't care about them, with the end result being painful and crushing. Does this sound familiar?

Some of us are natural caregivers. We often have a dream that our love will be enough or that we will be enough to inspire our partners to want to find a job, quit drinking, stop cheating or lying. We want to help them be more confident and get over their fear of commitment. Women and men stay in unfulfilling relationships that are fueled by rescue fantasies. In reality, it is very rare for this kind of relationship to be successful because it is too one-sided. When the one rescued feels whole again, professional experience has shown it is doubtful they will want to spend their time with someone who reminds them of how broken they were before. These people move on, leaving the rescuer confused and resentful.

Worse yet, they remain always broken, and you remain always the caretaker. That will get very old and leave you feeling both alone and drained.

A healthy relationship is based on two healthy individuals that possess the ability to give and take. You may have already put two, five or ten years into a one-sided relationships hoping for a return on your investment. I guarantee you that you are much more likely to get two, five or ten more years of the exact same thing. Let's say you help the person get healthier, cleaner, wiser, employed, etc. My experiences in counseling have shown there is a reason that those relationships usually end bitterly as well. Why you ask? Because oftentimes no one wants to be reminded of the failure or drain they once were, and your presence does exactly that.

In clearing the deck, there are essentially three steps:
1.) Clear your life of messy relationships
2.) Clear and clean your physical house
3.) Clear out the mental negativity (use what works for you)

Cleaning up your physical house is actually another mental and visual imagery exercise you do physically to prepare your life for the positive change you want to bring into it. Since every day is a possible day for this person to come into your life, you always have to be ready. It is time to get rid of all the clutter and, while you are at it, rearrange some items, leaving empty spaces for the new person's stuff. When your environment is in order, your brain will be less stressed and more relaxed.

This exercise will help you deal with the empty time you have created by ridding your life of messy activities, 'going nowhere' relationships and meaningless things. As you are clearing the clutter, imagine what will be created in the empty spaces. Get rid of what anchors you in the past or put it away. If you have a place to store it, or can afford to rent a storage space, put the things there. If you can't do either of those things, or don't want to, is there a way you can confine that doll collection to one room where you display your favorites and carefully store the others in a closet?

Think about this new person, what will make your space look more inviting and comfortable to them? Physical cleanliness is essential. A place for them to put their things is imperative for them to be able to imagine sharing the space with you. Even if your hope is to eventually move into someone else's space, if your space is overflowing that suggests to a future partner you will also be too much to deal with in their space. Clutter suggests chaos, and healthy people usually don't to want bring that type of lifestyle into their home.

Mentally getting your house in order, like so many of the other steps outlined herein, is an ongoing process that never is finished. However, there are certain aspects of this that have to be addressed first. If you never believe it will happen, then it certainly will not. Even if you were to meet this right person, how would you recognize they fit your requirements? There are certain aspects of your wish list that are non-negotiable, but there are others that are not needed for you to be happy and content.

This is a good time to go back and look at your initial list of what you are looking for in a relationship. Negativity attracts negativity, and you are trying to create something positive in your life. Rewrite your list now using only positive statements. If you are used to thinking in negativities this will be somewhat difficult and require practice. Most people who are unhappy are so used to thinking and feeling badly that they have no idea they are even doing it. It is essential to address this in order to feel happier and create a more fulfilling life.

Training yourself to think in more positive ways is part of the process of learning Cognitive Behavioral Therapy (CBT) techniques. CBT involves thinking positively in the present moment. What we think determines how we feel, and we can change our thoughts to feel more optimistic and positive. Let's look at some examples of how you would do this. Examine your list and determine if the descriptions of characteristics you are looking for is stated in positive tones or as negative traits you are trying to avoid. Rewrite the negative statements into positive ones. Here are some conversion examples:

Examples of negative partner requirements versus positive partner requirements:

He/She can't be fat	vs.	He/She should be of a normal weight and/or well proportioned
He can't be bald	vs.	He will have some hair or a shaved head
He/She can't be frigid or cold	vs.	He/She will like closeness/affection
He/She can't be a gold digger	vs.	He/She will be working towards a career or success
She can't have short/long hair	vs.	She will be open to changing her hairstyle to one I might prefer
He/She can't be stingy/greedy	vs.	He/she has a generous heart
He/she can't be controlling	vs.	He/She believes in compromise

Step Four: Rewrite your list of requirements and desires using only positive statements, then throw the old list away. The old list doesn't serve your goals, and is getting in the way of you reaching them.

CBT Thinking Points:
* You have to believe that this can happen in order for it to happen.
* You have to create the space for it to happen.
* You have to release your negativity and replace it with positive thoughts in order to let it happen

Visualization for a clearer living space:

Imagine yourself once again in your comfort place. Look around the room. Is everything just where you put it? Isn't it lovely that everything has its place and it is where you expect it to be? Now imagine another room in your living space that you've been meaning to clear out. Look at specific areas of this room where you know you have piles of clutter. Maybe it's a stack of junk mail catalogues you never get around to looking at. Now picture yourself saying "I don't have time to look at these and I don't need to buy more stuff. Let me put them in a bag to recycle them."

Go around this room and imagine what it will look like cleared, with everything put away, given away, thrown away or donated. How does it feel now to be in this space? Does it feel much more comfortable now? Do you feel a sense of satisfaction that you accomplished your goal? Do you find the newly created open spaces inviting?

Affirmation for organization:

"I can make quick and efficient decisions about what to keep, and what to throw away or give away, and I enjoy being able to find things right where I know they will be. I will release my attachment to things I really don't need."

two

Finding Your Partner, Where to Look?

It's an amazing world out there with the options both overwhelming and even frightening at times. Before you venture out of your immediate life sphere, look first at your own life, where you go every day and what you do. I have a cousin who when single was able to meet interesting potential partners everywhere she went, and I mean everywhere. She wasn't that much more attractive than I was yet I couldn't figure out how she did it. Most of the men she dated were rich, attractive and madly in love with her. She worked an office job and had a seemingly average life? How did she keep finding them? What did she have that I didn't?

I had to spend more time with her to find out the answer was remarkably simple in principle. Simply, she had the ability to meet people's eye contact and smile wherever she was. As a result, she met people everywhere she went. As we have all heard, a smile is understood in every language. This simple act afforded her the opportunity to meet many potential partners from which to choose. When the choices are vast it is just one more step in the process to weed out the wrong ones and select the ones with the most potential. She likely had to turn a lot of people down, which I am sure was pretty uncomfortable at times. We never talked about how she handled those situations but I am sure she learned how to do so with relative ease.

How do you find them? I have a theory that we pass by potential partners every single day and many worthy candidates are right under our noses. After you have cleared some time and space in your life to meet someone, look up and around. Look up because too many of us are so consumed with our problems, thoughts, smart phones and activities we miss so much of what is happening around us. Look around because your everyday world may indeed have legitimately good prospects you haven't noticed yet.

Where do you see people? Are there people at work with whom you are friendly? Are any of them friendly enough to ask if they might have a friend they could introduce you to? Might one of them be someone you wouldn't mind getting to know better? Are there any people you pass at work, see in the elevator or buy lunch from that catch your eye? Are they single?

So first, let's look at how you are currently spending your time. How much time are you spending with people you don't want to be with doing things you don't really have to do? Look at your friendships and family relationships. What kinds of people do you really enjoy being with? What kinds of activities do you like doing? Is there anything you can do in your current daily life to make a space for a new friend? It is going to take time to be with this new person. Therefore, you may have to do some prioritizing of your time.

I want to share with you a mistake another friend of mine, Cathy, has repeated for years. She has lots of rules about finding a partner, about when they should call and how they should act. She has a habit of keeping herself very, very busy. She is afraid of feeling too lonely and alone to leave free time in her schedule. If Cathy does meet someone, what do you think his inner thoughts are about the fact that it will take three weeks for her to have time to see him again? When you meet the person who you would like to spend more time with, if you are never free to make this happen, to spend time with them and see if they are right for you, a smart person will go look somewhere else. Healthy people know their time is valuable too!

This also works the opposite way. If the person you have convinced yourself is a worthy prospect doesn't make you a priority and find the time to be with you, then it's probably time to let that one go. If you are not important enough for them to make spending time with you a priority, than you are wasting your time. Those kinds of relationships are mostly based on you spending time thinking about them, not vice versa. They are not unlike internet relationships where people convince themselves they will get married to someone they have never even met or spent actual time with. There is real danger to the fantasies we can create in that void where one-on-one interaction should occur.

I see people convince themselves that these are real relationships all the time. They are not real relationships! They are fantasies and fantasies are always wonderful, but fantasies won't keep you warm at night. It is fine to meet people online, but the actual meeting needs to take place sooner rather than later. I wouldn't give any of these internet opportunities more than a month before the actual meeting takes place. Otherwise the danger is that you have a wonderful relationship with your fantasy and no relationship with a real person.

REAL RELATIONSHIPS ARE the ones SPENT FACE-TO-FACE!

Be a person you feel good about, one worthy of having a good relationship. Find a person who is worthy of being in a relationship with you.

I worked with a very attractive young woman named Maureen. She would meet guys, give them her number then end up frustrated waiting for them to call. This caused her a great deal of discomfort because she wanted to know quickly if they were interested in her or not. After this happened to her a number of times I asked her for more details about the types of conversations she was having with the men she was meeting. Turns out when they did suggest getting together she was frequently busy. She didn't realize her unavailability was sending the wrong message to the very candidates she was actually interested in.

We discussed whether some of her plans were flexible, and since most of them were, I suggested she try whenever possible to be available for dates when asked, or to consider offering an alternative 'get together plan'. Being aware of how hard it is for one person to reach out to another, if you are truly busy that day it's important to offer an alternative meeting time so the person knows you are interested.

When Maureen started taking herself out of the usual female dating role and become more transparent about her interest, she was able to find out if the suitor's interest was sincere. Additionally, she spent much less time alone, wondering whether someone was interested or not, waiting for them to call. She successfully transitioned her life to spending more time with people who really wanted to get to know her.

In my daily work it amazes me how many very attractive, intelligent and wonderful people are alone. Not by choice mind you, but because they don't take any time to think about it, or feel too afraid of being rejected to reach out. Many wonderful people have been hurt or rejected so many times they have just given up. Try to keep in mind you are only looking for one good relationship, just one person. It won't happen by hoping or magic. Everything you have right now in your life is because you set a goal and worked to achieve it. Finding a good partner is something you will have to work at if this is what you truly want.

How do you start finding out if a person is available and might be interested in you? First, you have to think about where you see this person, along with a topic of conversation. Mundane as it is, people often start conversations by talking about the weather or commenting on a situation in their life. The art of conversation is somewhat of a lost art because so many people communicate mostly by text, email, etc.; yet the basics of conversation include asking open ended questions about which people feel comfortable. If there is something interesting about the weather, in the news, or a holiday coming up, asking people their opinions on those things will give you a lot of information about their views and availability.

A good way to start a conversation is to mention something you like, enjoy or are interested in; asking the person what they think about it. Be prepared to move to a new topic if the first one doesn't go anywhere or you get an awkward response. Sound interested in what they are telling you! Watch their body language and yours. If they don't make eye contact and face away, they are not interested or you've picked a bad time to approach them. If your body language actually communicates your fear, it may be misconstrued as disinterest. Try to face the person, make eye contact, and try to smile. Practice with people all around you whom you have absolutely no interest in until you get more comfortable. As with anything, you will get better and more comfortable with practice.

The second way to meet someone is to widen your activity circle. Join some special interest groups, take a class or explore volunteering. If you take a class, join a book club or a fitness group you may find something you really enjoy and meet people too. Years ago, in an effort to get to know my future stepdaughter better I handed her a brochure from the local art center and told her to pick a class she was interested in attending with me. It turned out to be a clay class and I loved it! Working with clay has now been a great passion of mine for over fifteen years! Who knew the goal of spending more time with someone would give me the unexpected gift of a lifelong hobby?

Every community has a plentitude of opportunities for volunteering. Volunteering involves having a common task, which provides for an easy way to meet people and feel comfortable while doing so. Whenever you volunteer somewhere you will have another thing about yourself to feel proud of, and, in turn, that will help your confidence and self-esteem build. Here is the great thing about giving, even if you don't meet anyone you become a better person! It is a win/win situation any way you look at it.

Finally, if you have looked up and around you with clear vision and determined there is no one remotely interesting, and you have tried all these options, and still can't think of any activities you would enjoy - then why not consider using the internet or a dating service?

The internet can be dangerous for a number of reasons: it is full of people who believe magic is possible with little or no real effort, it is full of professional predators and it is very easy to lie when hiding behind a computer screen. Many of the people you might come across are those to be avoided, and that can be daunting.

Because of those risks, before you join any Internet dating site, you should set up a separate email account that you use only for this purpose. Also, I strongly suggest you consider purchasing a pay as you go phone. Additionally, let's face it – identity theft is very real and has serious consequences. Early on in any internet relationship I think you should be very wary of sharing any personal information before you have met the person face-to-face. It goes without saying that money or gifts should never be given to anyone you have never met.

If you are using the Internet, you must use it as a means of screening potential candidates for You! It can be a very useful tool in finding other people looking for that special someone because of the number of potential people available to you. Be active! If you post a profile and wait for responses to seek you out, it will likely result in more people who are wasting your time. If you are going to use the Internet to meet people, below are some suggestions I have to help you make good decisions about whom to meet and whom to avoid.

Practical Internet Dating Suggestions:

1.) Establish a separate email address for internet dating
2.) Purchase a pay as you go phone
3.) Use a flattering but current and realistic picture of yourself
4.) Be clear that you are looking for a serious relationship and not a friend or someone to have fun with. Don't respond to people who indicate that is what they are looking for
5.) Ask the person how recent their picture is
6.) Seek out the people you are interested in and be very selective, smart and cautious about the ones that choose you
7.) Wait no longer/chat no more than a couple of weeks before meeting. If the person is not available over and over, lose that contact
8) Choose people who are geographically realistic to meet with

The Internet dating experience has created a new opportunity to meet people while also creating a new type of problem. People have met via the internet and webcams and begin to think they are in a relationship. Soon after, they begin creating in their minds all the aspects of a real relationship, even getting to the point of discussing marriage without ever meeting the person. Some of these pseudo relationships have begun to be exposed in the media, but the problem is that they result in all the pain of a real breakup.

It's very easy for a person who engages in lots of magical thinking and fantasy about finding love to create the same magical thinking and fantasy about an internet "relationship". Many of these people have turned out to be nothing like they have portrayed themselves to be yet the hurt and pain they cause is very real. An example of how seriously these false relationships are taken by the people in them is the recent story in the media about a teen who killed herself after her internet "boyfriend" turned on her and became very mean. The "boyfriend" turned out to be a parent of a child who competed with this girl in cheerleading.

Recently, the "Doctor Phil" show portrayed three women who had extensive and years long "relationships" which turned out to be not with a man at all, but a pathologic woman portraying herself that way! Each of those women felt they were in a real relationship and each of them devoted their hearts, minds, time and hard earned money before they finally gave up. Every time they were going to meet 'he' came up with some dramatic emergency that took place and cancelled. Each of them perceived this as a sad ending when they finally gave up, and the predator moved on. Each of them had their hearts severely damaged.

We all live in our own minds, and the void of being with a person leaves lots of room to fantasize, which can be dangerous to your mental well-being. The way to avoid building up a mental relationship is simple. Meet the person as soon as possible. If you don't actually spend time with a person, in person, then you are not really getting to know them. Think back on your own life, can you think of other instances where you thought you really knew someone until, say, you lived with them? This can happen with great friends who become roommates and after living together for a year the friendship is shattered. Liking a person and being able to live comfortably with them are two very different things, so it requires an extensive amount of time spent together to make a good decision.

Even with marriages, and those who live together for years without marrying, things change. There is a certain part of us that always puts our best foot forward and doesn't truly relax into our real self until we feel totally safe. Let's all admit it's not only our partner, but we do it too! We all have a hidden side and wonder if the imperfections that exist within make us unlovable.

Further, we are all afraid of the rejection that may come if these characteristics of ours drive off a potential partner. Yet, the reality is that we're better off being as transparent as possible as early as possible in a relationship. If the person can't accept those flaws, then they aren't ready for a serious relationship with you.

I am not trying to minimize the pain of a failed relationship, the time it takes to process the loss and the enormous effort involved in starting again. You will need to pamper yourself for a little while, examine your life and your choices, figure out what you can learn from it, rest and then move on when you're ready.

As a therapist I can't say this strongly enough: Don't go from one relationship right into another! It's important to be able to tolerate some pain. As bad as it feels, it won't kill you. It's important to be able to let yourself deal with the pain of the loss. Part of being ready to be in a healthy adult relationship is that you have to do everything you can to be one half of that healthy adult relationship. Being able to tolerate and handle pain is an important skill for enduring the hardships of life and relationships.

Pain is frightening and overwhelming! But pain and the feelings that come with it will not kill you! Practicing how "to be with your feelings" without always reacting to them is an important component in having a successful, mature and healthy relationship.

We have three instinctual responses when we are overwhelmed: fight, flight or freeze. It is normal that we have those but necessary to identify the one that you are probably overusing in your life and examine it. If you are constantly driven by the fear response, you will have problems functioning in a lot of aspects of your life and may need to spend some time with a therapist to help you see how your overuse of this instinct is negatively affecting your life.

The problem with our fear responses is that these instincts were once extremely important for our survival as humans but interfere tremendously with our ability to handle stress and intimacy in a very stimulating world. Your fear response can cause you to overreact and end a relationship that could have a lot of positives for your life. This whole process of meeting a new person and trying to have a healthier and more supportive relationship is very frightening. In fact, just the meeting part is overwhelming. As hard as it can be, observe your fear and don't do anything to change how you feel, just don't act on it either. Observe it, and let it be.

Try not to react and allow yourself to feel this fear. Accept it as natural. Breathe! The key is to develop coping skills, methods and ways that allow the fear to dissipate! So through the process of accepting the experience, learning to breathe and live through your pain and fear, you are doing one of the most important steps necessary to ready yourself for a healthy relationship and a successful life. This is imperative because as you meet new people, you are going to be deciding early on whether this person could be a suitable partner for you, and since most of them may not be suitable, you will have to face your fears and move on.

To some extent, your early meetings should be viewed somewhat as job interviews wherein you are the employer. When you find out some details about the person that definitely are on your "not negotiable" list, and you're already wondering if you can give up or negotiate on this detail you've already defined as very important, it is time to face the reality this is not a person with which you want to pursue that kind of relationship. Remember, you already identified how important certain traits are so don't compromise.

If the person always has to reschedule or postpone, after two or three of these STOP, you are done! Move on. You don't have the time to waste repeating the same mistakes! PERIOD, THE END! Further, you have to call THE END very quickly when you know it's wrong. Don't continue spending time with someone thinking you didn't give them enough of a chance.

Maybe, maybe, maybe – STOP having a relationship in your mind. Those are pleasant, but not real.

I am not saying you shouldn't be willing to amend some parts of your list of must requirements. You might find someone worth giving up one trait because most of the others do meet your criteria. But as you meet people that list of qualities you made in chapter one is important! Be sure the trait you are willing to accept is a minor one, not one of the 'absolutes'! When you come home after spending time with a person look at your list to evaluate if the person has the requirements you are looking for or not.

Remember the cousin I talked about earlier? The one who meet men everywhere? One of the things that will happen when you start meeting a lot of people is that you will have to walk away from many meetings when you quickly realize they don't have the qualities you are looking for in a relationship. She has had to turn down quite a few men, which I am sure was pretty uncomfortable at times. We never talked about how she handled those situations but I am sure she learned how to do so with relative ease.

Just like with her, around you are some interesting single people. Start out by asking them how they say no to inquiries they are not interested in. Like anything else you learn, it will take some practice to become comfortable and competent. It's easier to begin conversations with people you have no interest in romantically just to get practice with starting conversations. As you expand your practice to beginning conversations with a person who could be a romantic partner, prepare yourself for how you want to handle your exit from the conversation as well. Ask others in your circle of influence that are in committed relationships how they handle it when they are approached by people they aren't interested in. Figure out in advance some statements you can make to comfortably exit these situations.

Saying no comfortably is a problem many people have. Our instincts often tell us when something is wrong, and because it is so uncomfortable to say no, we waste tons of time with people who that, in the end, are a waste of our time. Our time is our most valuable possession and we want to be spending it with quality partners and friends. It is infinitely easier to end a relationship earlier than later, a subject that will be addressed in more detail in Chapter 3 on Ending Bad Relationships.

Having a handful of comments prepared will make it easier for you to let people know you are not interested in pursuing the relationship further before the conversation gets too awkward. Let's say you're in a coffee shop, the barista is cute and flirting with you. Or you have struck up a conversation with someone on the bus, but you find out that they are in the process of getting divorced, are unemployed or you discover another piece of information that sends up a red flag. I am assuming you are reading this book because you've already wasted too much time making one bad choice after another. You have already decided you don't want to waste any more time so let's not waste energy on people who aren't ready right now. Save yourself the grief and frustration. By having a set of comments you can throw into the conversation to ease out of the situation you will find the exit much easier to pull off.

Here are a few I have found particularly helpful. You can come up with your own, but be ready with some before you get started. Remember, the goal is to make the person lose interest or to exit the conversation without hurting their feelings or unnecessarily embarrassing them. And you want to do so without opening yourself up to an argument.

1.) If I weren't married/engaged...
2.) I would like to see you but my live-in boyfriend might not be too happy about it. Thank you for your interest though
3.) It was so nice to meet you. Unfortunately, it's too bad I'm moving to Florida/Arizona next week because my parents need me to take care of them.
4.) While I enjoyed talking with you I am in a committed relationship. However, I have a sister who is single and very shy and I'm always

looking for someone to fix her up with. She is rather shy due to her weight issues, but if you are looking for someone I would love to fix you up with her.

5.) My partner Judy and I (same sex partner) were just talking about that the other day

6.) That sounds really nice but I am going to be busy with a heavy work project for the next 6 months that is important to my career, can I get your phone number and call you when the dust finally settles?

7.) I am flattered by your interest, but I am in a relationship

8.) Break eye contact, change the subject or talk about your many cats and how much you love them. Bring up your elderly Mom who lives with you and is bitter about your Dad.

9.) I am at the point in my life where I'm looking for a serious relationship or I am not interested in a serious relationship right now. Whichever you feel will be less interesting to them….then, if they argue, great, 'give me your number'

10.) I had this assignment for my psychology class to strike up conversations with strangers. This was very productive for me. Thanks for your help! Bye!

This is my list. Prepare your own. Writing things down is a way to practice them in your mind. You might find some of my suggestions comfortable for you and others no good. Make your own list NOW of ones you feel would be easiest to say and stay true to your character. Have at least three or four options minimum. Imagine yourself saying them. This mental exercise will be helpful when you employ some of these strategies later.

Use your imagination to create situations and predicaments where you need to use some of your escape expressions in order to be prepared for surprises. Make sure you keep this list with your other lists and always close by when you're out in a public setting with a potential partner. By having a list of exit tactics ready and practicing them beforehand you will feel much stronger when it is time to actually use one of them!

Women are always giving their numbers out and then never hear from the asker. We are somehow always surprised and hurt by this, but this is actually one of the easiest ways to extract yourself from an awkward situation. Men are very comfortable with using this deception. When you meet a man in a bar or in a situation where there is instant attraction, they may be speaking to you in the moment from that place of physical attraction. The only thing that happens in that moment is acknowledgment of the attraction.

You might be looking for a relationship. They might be looking for a hookup. You've already let them know you aren't interested in that. So it's logical you will never hear from them! Asking for someone's number is actually a terrific exit strategy employed by many.

This is your life, not a movie! Magic, fantasy and love at first sight rarely occur. Sustained love doesn't happen without time and effort. Practice saying no. When you don't hear from a prospective partner again, be grateful more of your time and effort hasn't been wasted with someone who doesn't want what you want. We are often taught that we should be agreeable and non-confrontational, because it isn't nice. Get over it! Say NO!

You can't be caught up with people who are a waste of time because if you are you won't have the time to spend with someone worthwhile when you meet them. Worse, they might interpret your lack of availability as a brush-off or game playing and walk away, leaving you wondering and confused over a lost opportunity.

Where is that list? This list is your vision, your guidebook – your compass. You need to have it out and refer to it regularly. When you meet someone and go out with them, or if you are looking for someone to meet on the internet, that list needs to be available and you need to reference it often to determine if the qualities you are looking for are present or not each time you read a profile or finish a date.

When you are lucky enough to actually meet and go out with someone, before you go further, take out that list and evaluate the person. Is this someone you might be able to spend the rest of your life with? Is your list similar to what the other person is looking for too? Does their behavior reinforce what they say? Remember, actions always speak louder than words. After many years in the therapy profession I HAVE FOUND A PERSON'S BEHAVIOR DEMONSTRATES MUCH MORE ABOUT WHAT IS IMPORTANT TO THEM THAT WHAT THEY SAY.

When you are feeling confused about their behavior or your feelings, those are red flags that this is not the 'one' you are looking for. You need to be aware of a number of red flags and recognize them quickly so you don't waste your precious time on people that will never be able to give you the emotional safety and security you are looking for.

Many of these people are loveable, worthwhile individuals who could be capable of being in a lasting relationship with you. But it will likely be some time before this could be true, thus going in you need to be aware you are taking a gamble. How many more years of your life are you willing to gamble away with no results? The answer depends on how old you are and what you are looking for in a relationship. You are the only one who can answer this. It is your life and your choice, so make this choice consciously and regularly.

Visualization Five for finding a partner:

Imagine yourself with your future partner. Try to imagine some of the physical features they have. Imagine how it feels to hug and be hugged by them. Imagine how it feels safe sharing your real opinions, hopes, dreams and fears. And listening to theirs! Imagine how it feels to take a walk together. Imagine sharing your favorite vacation spot with them and maybe even some of the activities you will do together while there.

Imagine different places you might meet this person and imagine how the conversation will start and how it will go. Imagine how later you might share the story of how you met, with others, maybe even your children one day, and how you will laugh about it.

Affirmation for finding a happy relationship:

"I know in my heart that there is a person out there who wants to be with me and who will complement my life! Someone that will appreciate who I am and unconditionally love me! I Believe I will find it."

three

Avoiding and Ending Bad Relationships

If you are reading this book, you may have just come out of a bad relationship. It is extremely hard to get out of a bad relationship, and having just experienced the pain they can cause, I'm sure you would prefer to avoid one in the future. Please give yourself time to evaluate and heal before you start the next relationship.

Sometimes thinking about past situations and how they turned out can help you to avoid similar situations if you can recognize those red flags sooner. If you rush from one relationship to another, there is no time to learn about and/or from what worked and what didn't. Let's discuss a few common red flags to watch out for so you can be more aware of what future issues could occur.

Some examples of Red Flags to watch out for:

1.) The person can only find time to spend with you outside of weekends or evenings, they keep rescheduling meetings and can only find blocks of time to get together

2.) The person is dating many people

3.) Someone who has been married three or more times

4.) Someone forty five or over who has never been married

5.) Someone whose life is in transition: ending another relationship, job transition, recent family death or moving

6.) Someone whose life is not stable

7.) History of addictions, arrests or infidelity

8.) The relationship is going unusually fast, the person is unusually eager to take it to the next step of living together, marriage, etc and you're feeling rushed

9.) Items on your own non-negotiable list are present

10.) You have distinctly different feelings about lifestyle, money, sex, family or how you handle stress and conflict

11.) You love him but hate his/her family or they dislike/disapprove of you

12.) You love them but don't like them

13.) The person has strong opinions and/or strict rules about your conduct or appearance

We have already helped prepare your avoidance tools. You completed your personal qualities list in Chapter One. In Chapter Two you made your list of exit strategies and excuses. In this chapter, we will review qualities that can be read flags. I will provide you my list and at the end you will use this as the basis for your own list of red flags. You will have three lists at the end of this chapter; these lists form the foundation of your new plan to finally find the right partner.

Keep all three handy, read and think about them regularly. A good time might be just before you go to sleep at night, or before you go out on a date. Having a clear image of what your looking for will help you recognize it when you find it. When you recognize this date isn't it, with practice you will be prepared to exit seamlessly and quickly. The easiest way to minimize bad relationships is to recognize them early, then end them quickly using your lists to guide you. This will be hard until you have practice, but it's kind of like taking a band-aid off a wound – faster is better!

When I first started this process and made a personal decision to no longer spend months and years dating people I would never consider marrying it shocked a lot of people I had been seeing on and off for years. I told one person I was engaged. I told another man I was seeing I made a commitment to a year of celibacy to improve my spiritual life. I told some people I won't be seeing them again. I think this is much easier done over the phone, by email or text. Having to say this face to face with someone can be difficult. I remember telling one man that I had decided I wanted to get married and he was not someone I would marry. It probably would have been nicer if I hadn't told him the actual truth as he looked totally shocked, yet I wanted to be honest with him. However, I might have also done him a favor, by not wasting his time and perhaps helping him to avoid a similar mistake in the future.

In some instances, you have to be ready to tell them why you are breaking off the relationship. It is up to you how you want to handle it. I think there's a lot of difficult but really eye opening information we can share with another person by being honest with them regarding the reason you are ending a relationship. It can indeed be looked at as a gift to do this with somebody. You need to determine if they both deserve and can handle the truth. The vast majority of people never take the time to tell another person the truth. Most people end relationships with no explanation, feedback or even a discussion. Think back to when this may have happened to you and then reflect on how it made you feel. The internet and text age has made this very easy to do, and there's nothing wrong with taking this route today. But I caution you to remember the 'Golden Rule' when possible.

Overall, remember the band-aid philosophy when it comes to breaking off a bad relationship and end it as early as possible. The earlier you do it the less time they have to become too attached. Do yourself a favor by keeping the list you developed before in the book of comments to use when fending off a suitor you are not interested in handy for these situations. Add a few of your own to the list.

If you have decided early on a person is either throwing out red flags, is stimulating your fear response much too often, or something just doesn't feel right to you, then it's ok to trust yourself and let the relationship end.

On the other hand, if you have found someone wonderful who meets all your criteria and you are still freaking out, then maybe it's time to consider therapy. Slow the relationship pace down and find a therapist you can discuss your fears with. If you are in a bad relationship and having a problem ending it, then this would be another excellent time to get some professional therapy – if only for the support factor! Bad relationships can span from bothersome to downright dangerous, and ending them can be very challenging. Seeking professional help is a terrific way to find a source of reinforcement and encouragement, along with working on issues that may be holding you back from your best self.

So to summarize some of the information we've covered so far, the key to avoiding bad relationships is to identify them early on before you've invested too much of your time and emotion. The more time, sacrifice and emotion you invest, the more time it will take for you to heal and be ready to move on. Since most failed relationships throw off signs early on, learn to recognize the red flags and keep track of them. If you identify four or more red flags within the first month of seeing someone new, it is a good idea to cut your losses and end it.

Ultimately, please think of these examples as suggestions rather than absolutes. They are here for you to become more thoughtful about the presence of these characteristics. Use what is helpful for you and discard the rest.

Let's review some of the red flags we have covered so far, why they may exist, and maybe, add some of your own to this list based on your experiences.

Red Flags that a relationship should be ended quickly:

The person can only find time to spend with you outside of the weekends or evenings.

Why: *The person does not physically have the time available for a relationship to develop. This red flag can also have exceptions, such as someone who has shared custody of their children and might only be available every other weekend. The best plan of action here is to observe what the priority is for that person when they have free time. If there are still very small windows to get together and you rarely seem to be a priority, this is a "no".*

The person reschedules your first or second meeting multiple times or is dating many people at once

Why: *This person is not physically available for your relationship to develop. Nor are they as interested in you as you are in them. Stop pursuing them and see if they pursue you. Give them a week or two, then lose their contact information and move on.*

The person can only find odd blocks of time to meet with you, over and over again, after one month. They are never available on weekends, evenings or holidays

Why: *Most likely this person is involved in another relationship and you are a little something on the side. While it's normal for the first few meetings to be at odd times, after a couple meetings the person is either interested in* *you or they're not. Again, a good test is to stop contacting them and let them contact you if they are available. If they continue to contact you with odd meeting times, then you can be sure you are not at the top of their list, or worse, something on the side.*

The person is dating many people

Why: *There is nothing wrong with dating multiple people when you are searching for a partner. But it is interesting to find out what the person doing it has in mind. If the person is doing this as an initial technique to meet a lot of people, there is no problem. So, you want to ask the person how long they have been doing this. If the answer is they have dated multiple people for years, this person is not really interested in an exclusive committed relationship.*

Someone who's been married three or more times

Why: *If 50% of marriages today end in divorce, then it is not at all unusual to be married more than once. If a person has been married three or more times, obviously they haven't figured out what they are doing wrong, or there is something wrong with their selection process. Divorce is emotionally draining and financially costly. You don't want to be number four do you????*

Someone over 45 who has never married

Why: *Someone this age who has never been married will likely never be married because this really isn't what he/she wants. They are either too unwilling to compromise or too picky when it comes to partners. This rule can also have an exception, such as a person who has been in a very long standing relationship without legal papers. However, if you meet someone this age that has never had a relationship longer than at least a year in their life, there is a good reason. Either they don't want one, they are impossible to get along with or impossible to please!*

The person's life is in transition: The person is unemployed, has been unemployed at least twice in the last year or has had three or more jobs in the last five years

Why: Our careers are a reflection of our ability to commit and get along with others in close relationships. In my experience both professionally and personally, people who are chronically unstable in their professional lives invariably require a lot of rescuing in their personal lives. And you may find yourself paying all the bills too. People who have trouble with commitment to their work or other interests generally won't stay with the same partner either. They will cause lots of instability, drama and stress in your life. Do you really want that on your plate?

The person is still involved in some way with their ex and a lot of feelings still linger, they have just ended a relationship or are in the process of a messy divorce

Why: The person is not emotionally available to develop feelings for you as they are not emotionally free. You will end up doing a lot of rescuing, and rescuing is not the basis of a healthy relationship. There can be exceptions when there are not a lot of emotions involved. So, in these situations you have to observe if the person appears emotionally stable, happy and available. Otherwise, this is a "no".

Someone whose life is not stable: People who have just suffered a difficult personal trauma such as a family death, a job layoff or a personal injury

Why: This person's focus will be completely on himself /herself for a while. And frankly, it needs to be. You are meeting and spending time with someone whom is most probably not their true selves at the moment. While it's nice to be helpful and supportive, the person really needs some time to process and deal with their own situation before they can be healthy enough to go looking for a relationship. They are most assuredly going to behave in erratic and unusual ways until they solve their issues. Besides, you need to be careful not to spend a lot of time, energy and money nursing someone who could, in the end, look at you as a care-taker, not a partner.

History of addictions, arrests or infidelity

Why: *People can change, and most of us do. Each of us has skeletons in our closets and we know we have made some serious mistakes. We are capable of changing and improving ourselves, and many people with troublesome pasts go on to lead effective and healthy lives. That being said, some folks never get over their problems. Remember, these items are red flags to be aware of and you must watch for evidence that the person has truly changed. People with this kind of history can continue on the same path as before, with nobody knowing whatsoever because they are amazingly adept at bending the truth. In the case of someone with a history of addiction, your main concern is to find out how long ago the issue was.*

If it is within the last year, this is a big red flag to move along in your quest. The recovery process, along with the personality and character changes required to be successful, takes over a year to accomplish - at the minimum! A person with less than two years in recovery is still in this process, but if they have made it past the first year and are actively involved in treatment, then you might consider taking the gamble. Look for displacement of one addiction into another obsessive kind of problem.

Arrests and infidelity often come with addiction issues, and these are other circum-stances where you should be cautious. The main thing you have to evaluate is the char-acter of the person: do they seem truly remorseful, take ownership and responsibility for their problems versus just blaming their behavior solely on the addiction, someone else or another outside influence? Anyone but themselves! If a person doesn't own their behavior and their mistakes, then in the future they will blame someone else when they continue to make them; most likely this 'someone else' will be you!

In general, when a person tells you something or gives you an explanation and it doesn't all really add up, your gut is tugging at you, causing you to be more anxious and confused, it is likely there is a problem with character and truth. You have to stop trying to convince yourself that it's okay when your gut is telling you it isn't.

The relationship seems like a dream and it's going very, very fast

Why: There are examples we are all aware of wherein "love at first sight" and "they live happily ever after" happen, but usually this is exactly what it sounds like - a fairy tale! Most likely, this scenario is the script you have already been following, and it hasn't worked out so well. Instant attraction is an instinct that is hard to resist, but what men and women think about when they feel this attraction is very different. True and lasting love is what happens when you spend time with a person and you fall in love with their character, their kindness, their patience and their soul. This takes time and you have to get beyond the instant attraction to see it.

This is the reason when you are attracted to someone in this fashion you should never move very fast.

Until you can spend enough time to see what is beneath the surface you are excited, stimulated and thrilled - but you are not in love! This kind of love is "puppy love" and can grow into something else if it is given time. Beware of the person in a hurry to move in with you, get quickly engaged and/or become exclusive too fast. We are talking the rest of your life here.

While you are looking for your partner continue having a full and active life. It takes time for someone with a healthy self-esteem and life to make all the changes required when incorporating their life with yours. In my professional and personal experiences, someone in too much of a hurry is usually hiding something. This could be the kind of person who wants to take over your life, or wants you to be committed before you really know what you're getting into. It is okay to talk and hope that this becomes something that lasts forever, but in my experience patience pays off.

In the end, the more time you allow to really find out what your conflicts are and how you each handle them, the more you can tell if you will be happy and compatible over time.

The person has a quality on your non-negotiable list

Why: *Remind yourself of why you have put this item on your list. A good example might be that you've put on your list someone who has had addiction issues. Maybe your father, mother or previous partner had that addiction issue. You already know this situation brings up too many problems for you, gets overwhelming and is just too hard for you to deal with – well guess what, that's perfectly fine! Better for you to accept this and not put yourself in a situation where your past brings anxiety to your present.*

If you are hemming and hawing about a quality you know you can't deal with you are putting yourself in a situation that is going to be more work/effort than pleasant/fun. Relationships and life are challenging enough without looking for more stress. You are trying to rid your life of unnecessary pain and drama, right?

You have distinctly different feelings about lifestyle, money, sex, family or how you handle stress and conflict.

Why: *Successful relationships are hard to find and even harder to maintain. Past the attraction and the marriage is the day to day living together, and the more different you are the more conflict you will have. There will always be some conflicts: about how you spend your time both together and apart, how you handle your finances, how sexually compatible you are, how much time is spent with family and so on. You may have found a wonderful human being, but you still might have too many compatibility issues to move further into the relationship.*

No matter how wonderful they are day- to-day life and stress can have a way of destroying love over time. If you have truly incompatible tastes or lifestyles, and one person does all the compromising, this will evolve into anger and resentment over time. *The person can be wonderful, but the two of you can still be incompatible! Thoughtfully considering the relationship before you make any serious steps that are difficult to get out of can save you a lot of time, pain and heart break later.*

Let's look at lifestyle as an example. You are a person who loves to eat out and go dancing, but your partner is a homebody. This doesn't have to be a deal breaker as long as each of you can respect your differences and still balance out the time you spend together. And the partner doesn't resent you going out dancing with your girlfriends. If you respect each other and can talk with each other, you can negotiate a compromise that will work.

Another common situation is one person is very neat and organized while the partner is the opposite. You need to consider if this is a person who is willing to make some effort to help you be more comfortable or not. If the response instead is "you want it that way, you do it", you need to be willing to make all the effort to reduce the conflict. Knowing this is the case, how long do you think it will be before feelings of anger and resentment build inside? If your current partner makes little or no effort you need to recognize that you will be the one doing all the work in other aspects of the relationship too. My advice: Move on!

Money is a huge issue that causes a lot of problems with many couples. Couples often have different perspectives on dealing with money and financial difficulties can cause great amounts of stress in any relationship. If your partner talks a good game but the behavior and spending you see don't support it, then this is another red flag. Let's face it, finances are often a stress whether with or without partners. What one person considers an essential item may be very different from another.

Let me give you an example from my first marriage. I borrowed a significant amount of money from my parents on more than one occasion to consolidate our bills with the goal of paying off our credit card debt, thus lowering our monthly costs. Can you imagine how I felt when I paid off my parents, only to find that the credit card bills were right where they were before I started? How do you think I felt when this actually happened again, for the third time?

The person who is making most of the money, who is more organized and practical, should be the one managing the money. Really, I could only blame myself for letting it happen exactly the same way again because I was too busy to take over the finances and he was an "accountant".

Funny thing is it still took me a few years to learn my lesson! Later in life I had a friend managing my retirement account and this friend left the company, assuring me her former employer would still manage the account. Guess what, almost all the investments failed. Why? Because nobody was actually managing the account and it was never reassigned. So, you see, in the end it was really my fault. Laziness and busyness are not excuses for letting your finances become in peril. YOUR FINANCES ARE SOMETHING YOU NEED TO LEARN ABOUT AND SPEND TIME MANAGING TOGETHER AS A TEAM. YOU ARE BOTH RESPONSIBLE!

Then there is the sex issue. It is unlikely that your sex drives will match exactly and that your sex life will be perfect without some effort and work. It's not very romantic, but like every other aspect of your relationship, sex has to be something you can talk about. If you find early on that your partner has trouble talking about your sex life, or they are unwilling to listen to what you need, I suggest you take a closer look at the strength of your bond. Remember, mentally and spiritually healthy people are open to talking about things with others because they realize that is how relationships stay strong.

You love him but you hate his/her family or they dislike/disapprove of you

Why: *Unless his family lives hours and states away, when you marry someone you are marrying his/her family. Their family of origin tells you a lot about where this person came from and how they were raised. There are definitely many who survive and live healthy lives that have come from dysfunctional families. A dysfunctional family of origin is not a reason to reject a partner. That being said, it is important to pay attention to how you feel about their family and think about how much time you will be spending with them in your future.*

If holidays are very important to you and you feel they will be ruined by spending them with his/her family you need to be honest with yourself about how much stress this will cause and how much conflict this will raise between yourself and your partner.

If you go into a relationship thinking you will be able to help the person cut the ties, or secretly plan to do this for your own gain, you may be successful, but you will be hurting the person you are involved with, and this will take its toll on your relationship over time. Blended families often bring this additional stress with them and can be an overwhelming factor in a relationship, leading to its demise. There are lots of strong feelings about family ties and they can become a major issue that pulls you apart. You didn't do all this work just to have it all fail later. Go into a situation with your eyes open, making sure you can honestly live with it.

I remember in my first meeting with my first mother in law all she could do was talk about her older son, even taking out the older son's baby pictures, while nary a one of my future husband was shown. I knew right then there were serious issues with this woman, her relationships with her children and her ability to unconditionally love. On many occasions over the course of our marriage she created stress for us and there were lots of horrible, miserable holidays with her. I remember realizing at the time of our meeting something was seriously wrong. I negated the effect this would have on my day-to-day life in the future. I thought this was something I could easily deal with. Boy, was I wrong!

The part I was naïve about was how her behavior was a clue as to how my future husband would handle conflict. If I had waited long enough to find out more about that I could have saved myself a lot of misery! On the other hand, if I hadn't made that mistake and lived with it unhappily for so long, I wouldn't have gained the knowledge to find out how to do everything different the second time around, along with how to avoid those mistakes. What's more, this book would never have been written. So I am grateful for my mistake in many, many ways! That being said, I'm going to assume you prefer not to sacrifice 10 years of your life to find out these things for yourself.

You love them but don't like them

Why: *We all enter marriage hoping it will last a lifetime. Unfortunately, there is no such thing as a perfect life. Good and bad things happen; happiness and sadness befall us all. Hard times test every relationship, and this is when it will be extremely important to not only like your partner, but respect them too. Feelings of love will be strained during hard times. Sometimes you may not feel love at all. During those times, if you don't and respect each other, the marriage will fail.*

Real love is not based on fantasies. It is based on mutual respect, and you genuinely liking and respecting the person will be what sustains you through the hardest times. When people say their partner is their best friend, it means that this is someone who accepts you when you are at your best and worst. They don't turn on you because you made a mistake or acted inappropriately. They don't leave you because you gained 20 pounds either. True love looks past many things, especially if grounded in a deep, abiding sense of respect for the individual your partner is.

The person has very strong and strict rules about your conduct or appearance.

Why: *Everyone has quirks! We all have our certain ways of wanting to do things and that is normal. But there are many partners who give you cues before you get serious that they are inflexible on some subjects.*

If this is a subject such as monogamy, and you totally agree, then there is no issue. I think one of the most common "rules" I have come across, particularly in men, concerns the weight of the other partner. If they make derogatory comments about fat people or you hear them making negative comments about traits like weight, height or skin color in others, be prepared. Our bodies change as we age. Life stress and health issues can be some of the things that cause weight fluctuations. I have heard stories about men telling their partners they were ugly and fat when they were pregnant. If those women searched their memories, I suspect clues to that verbal abuse and intolerance were present before the pregnancy.

What seems like a quirk can become a major issue in a relationship. Your weight becomes their excuse for infidelity or ending the relationship, and it's "your fault". Someone with those rigid views sees a partner as an object, not a person, and is looking for a trophy, not a partner.

Ending Bad Relationships

Once you have come to the conclusion that this relationship is bad or unhealthy, you have to prepare for moving on. Leaving requires some preparation and you need to have a plan. It might be that you decide to wait for a specific date for some reason. It is often easier to begin making your plans before you announce them. But you need to be clear and honest with yourself. If you have come to the conclusion that the relationship you are in is unhealthy, you should try to end it as soon as possible. If it requires you moving out, you will have to find a place to go. It is likely you will be feeling insecure and vulnerable for a while, thus it would be helpful if you can arrange temporary accommodations with a good friend or family member who will support you in this decision.

You might want to work with a therapist who can help you plan your exit strategy. This can be very helpful for a number of reasons. RARELY IS ANY EXIT NEAT AND CLEAN! If you're honest about the reasons you can expect at minimum to get either an argument, a request for another chance or a promise of change. You may even have second thoughts when you're on your own and realize adjusting is harder than you thought. Once you've involved your family and friends they might get angry with you if you go back a few times, as does often occur, so working with a therapist is a good idea because a professional understands it can take several tries to make a successful change. They won't be angry if you fail the first few times. Regretfully, sometimes your friends and family will.

If the end signals your need to find a new place on your own, then begin to put money aside in a separate account or safe deposit box which will serve as a down payment on your new place. If you are ending an abusive relationship many cities have shelters with support in place for those looking to start a new beginning. You may want to contact your county to find out what resources are available to you. All of this depends on you preparing in advance the necessary steps to ensure the smoothest transition possible.

Actually saying the words "our relationship is over" to another person could be harder or easier than you imagine it will be. It's a lot like when you need to say no to a pushy salesperson trying to make a sale. The less information you give and the more you repeat "The relationship isn't making me happy and I have made the decision that it is time for us to go our separate ways" both to yourself, and to the other person involved, the easier it will be. You want to avoid giving reasons, because reasons give the person something to argue with you about, and usually those conversations are what got you in this situation in the first place.

No one knowingly enters a bad or abusive relationship. There is nothing broken or wrong with you because you are in this situation. There are a large number of unhealthy people in the world who feel the way to have a relationship is to have all the control and power over someone. The "victim" in an unhealthy or abusive relationship almost never knows how controlling the other partner is when they first become involved.

The predators and abusers in the world are adept at putting on masks to the outside world that casts them as wonderful and nice. That mask is what you first saw when you were attracted to them. Every time you forgave them when they wronged you, overlooked their flaws, accepted their accusations and/or believed it was entirely your fault - you got sucked into their unhealthy world deeper and deeper!

When you tried to leave but then went back, your family and friends probably became more estranged because they supported you, believed in your decision and were disappointed when you went back to the negative relationship. Try and remember it is because your family/friends love you and they don't understand the insidious ways of predators. Controlling partners are excellent at helping build walls between you and your support system. They don't want your family and friends to see what is really happening, so they work to create friction in order to provide distance between you and the very people who love you.

Being involved with a predator or abuser is a kind of seduction and can happen to anyone. Not to mention usually being much more difficult than other relationships to end. Getting out of one of these can be time consuming and costly, both financially and emotionally. Pain notwithstanding, it is certainly worth the trouble of getting out of any cycle of abuse.

You are too special and valuable, your life is too precious, to allow the relationship to continue. You will probably need some professional assistance to help you deal with the whole process. Books such as *"Stop Signs"* by Lynn Fairweather and *"How to Spot a Dangerous Man Before You Get Involved"* by Sandra L Brown are terrific resources to help you start the road to freedom.

Fortunately, the vast arrays of bad relationships are not that difficult to end. Most of the time you can look at the list of red flags and implement them:

- Be too busy, or busy working – it's very easy to tell someone you will call them, and then just don't or call and leave messages when you know they won't answer

- You're going out of town

- You're planning on moving in a few months and don't want to get that involved

- You got back with an old boyfriend/girlfriend and are getting engaged

- You're moving back in with your parents

- You lost your job and moved back in with an old boyfriend/ girlfriend

Let me be straight about something here. Being honest is nice, but sometimes it just isn't worth it! Most of the time, you will get an argument about any reason you give, and arguing is just a waste of energy. Besides, allowing them to try and talk you into investing more of your time and energy will just make the later ending messier. Most people with issues who aren't doing anything to change themselves aren't going to benefit from the truth, so just do whatever you have to do, breathe a sigh of relief and pat yourself on the back for not wasting months and years of your life!

Unhealthy people rarely have healthy reactions to bad news, especially when it has to do with their behavior. What I am saying is if you can foresee the break-up going badly because of the truth you might possess, simply hold onto that truth and don't share it.

The hardest part is making the decision and then seeing it all the way through. If you have taken the time to set the goals and identify the qualities you want in a relationship, if you are willing to do the work to find it, then this is something you can make a reality in your life. As a matter of fact, you are entitled to it! The sooner you stop accepting and making excuses for your partner or your own immature and unhealthy behaviors, the sooner you can find someone worth your time and effort.

Overall, always keep in mind when you stick to your game plan, look for the signals and slowly develop your relationships you will recognize much earlier the ones that won't bring happiness, thus making it easier to end them sooner before either of you are as emotionally invested.

Visualization for Blocking Negativity:

Imagine yourself standing in front of the person you are saying good-bye to. When you look at them, remember all the qualities about them that are bad for you or that you don't like, and imagine them written in big black and white block writing on a huge poster board covering the entire front side of their body. Every time they try and come up with an excuse, or move the blame to you, just continue to see the words in front of you – they will reinforce the reasons why you need to stay strong and not let their 'logic' break you down.

Or, imagine you are surrounded by loose bricks and mortar. Now begin picking up the bricks and use the mortar to build a physical wall around you. If they continue to 'reason' with, argue with or manipulate you, simply watch their words as they bounce off your brick wall and dissolve into the ground. If you already know some of the arguments they will present, imagine watching them speak the words but you can't hear them because they can't penetrate your wall. You are safe, secure and protected in your fortress. Prepare for showing no reaction to the other persons words, anger or frustration. This walled off perspective will help remove much of the emotional element out of the conversation.

Imagine this wall as present anytime you talk to them and their words bouncing off each and every time.

Affirmation for letting go:

"I release you with love into the universe. I am valuable, special and unique. I am open and ready for a new companion to come into my life that will appreciate and cherish me!"

four

Fear: When to Listen and When to Ignore It

Hopefully all the hard work you have done as directed in the first few chapters now has you in a position to entertain a new person in your life. Maybe you have already identified a possible candidate. Now what? Well, once you've checked your red flag list, your desirable traits list and you feel some degree of attraction or interest in this person, now you have to face your fears and establish contact. Our minds often do something that we don't consciously realize we're doing. We often imagine pain, rejection, failure and humiliation. This conscious or unconscious negative imaging in our minds can often create a lot of discomfort and tension within. Whether we realize it or not, all this negative imaging we participate in, even if done in the hopes of sparing ourselves future pain, many times ends up bringing into existence what we expect to happen, even contributing to it happening.

So this time you are going to do something you've never done before. Imagine success. We are more likely to bring success into our lives when we expect and imagine that good things will happen. We are more likely to bring success into our lives when we expect and imagine that good things will happen. When a person goes into a job interview expecting to be hired they convey a different energy than the one who goes in already believing nothing good will happen, so they are wasting their time. The person who enters with a positive expectation is more likely to get a positive result. Both personally and professionally I can say that the world reflects back to us what we put out.

For help on learning to face to your fears, I haven't found a book better than *"Feel the Fear and Do It Anyway"* by Dr. Susan Jeffers. This book was given to me by a friend while I was feeling overwhelmed by fear when the man who had all the qualities I dreamed of came into my life. While the "blocking negativity" visualization described at the end of the last chapter was one I invented to cope with my verbally abusive ex-husband, "Feel the Fear" was the source I used when dating my new husband. The gist of "Feel the Fear" is step-by-step positive thinking to face, tolerate and slowly conquer your fears. Remember that discomfort is a natural response to doing anything new. If you haven't felt it for a while, then you are probably doing the same things every day.

It's time to try something new! If you've already been hurt, already been betrayed, already felt destroyed and you are here now - you have already gotten through it! You know how to survive! If you already know how to survive and you're out there functioning in this crazy world, you already have a lot more guts and strength than you realize, so embrace it!

We are all born with three instincts which are there to protect us: fight, flight, and flee. The problem is that in today's society our brains are developing faster than our instincts can keep up with. The result of living in a demanding and stimulating society is we are constantly bombarded by sensory overload and, therefore, have absolutely no idea when our instincts should be paid attention to versus when should they be ignored. Two unfortunate things can result. First, we listen to our fears when they stand in the way of making changes to better our lives. Second, we don't face our fears when it would be good for our lives to do so, such as when we are afraid to end a bad relationship because we fear we won't find a new one.

While my sister and I were both going through divorces, we spent more than a few weekends together to support each other and adjust to this new found alone time on our hands. We usually got the free Chicago Reader newspaper, which is still distributed today, and would read all the personal ads on Friday nights, with a strong dose of giggling throughout. One day I read an ad I actually was very interested in. I didn't say anything, but I continued to think about it. About a month later, I shared this secret with my sister and said I wanted to respond to it, but I was too afraid at the time. It had taken me a month to even share with her that I was interested!

So I asked her to promise to make me call, or even make the call for me, if I saw the same ad appear again. I knew myself well enough to know that I wouldn't do it on my own, especially since my fears prevented me from telling her about it for a month. By saying it out loud I had made a commitment and also had her make one to me.

I continued to read the ads, with hope and trepidation the same ad might run again. Two months later it did, and this time I told her about it right away. I called and arranged to meet the man outside a multistory building close to work. We walked to a nearby restaurant and ate lunch. I was just emerging from an abusive relationship and I was terrified, but he looked very relaxed and calm. Since this was the second time he had posted his ad, I knew he tried this before, giving us a good topic to begin our conversation. He had lots of interesting, funny stories about some of his experiences. Dates that ordered two and three entrees, trying to get the most out of the free meal as possible (i.e. future meals for themselves) or how they would order the most expensive item on a menu. He was funny, he was calm and he was kind. He had entertaining stories about his children wanting him to "get a life" and I found myself feeling at ease with this man. I realized I had never felt this safe around a man before and I knew he was special.

I also felt terrified at the idea of getting involved with someone new!

My girlfriend Susie gave me the aforementioned book *"Feel the Fear and Do It Anyway"* by Susan Jeffers PhD. during this period. I was sure I would do something to sabotage the relationship because my anxiety was overwhelming me, to the point that I was physically shaking at times. The book and the approach developed therein to conquer fears helped me learn to control my responses and act in ways that supported positive, healthy decision-making processes. I wrote notes on whatever issue I was working on at the time, with the action steps I was taking to overcome those fears.

Even though my fear was so strong that I cried when walking down the aisle years later, I still did it knowing I was doing the right thing for myself despite what my irrational fears where saying. Surprisingly, when I talk about it now, very few people who attended the wedding knew I was crying at the time. My husband says "I knew you were crazy when I married you", but he says it in a loving way. We have the normal ups and downs of every relationship, but I am very happy about taking that risk, with over eighteen years together so far.

With the variety and multitude of ways to meet someone comes the same plethora of ways we can get ourselves involved with a partner who is dangerous or unscrupulous. The internet as a way to meet someone is also an opportunity to look at the profile from a critical standpoint. The danger is if we let our fantasies color our reality. A perfect partner who sounds too good to be true often is too good to be true. A way to keep yourself grounded when searching the internet for a potential partner is to have a trusted friend help you screen applicants.

A friend can point out to you when you're ignoring your profile deal breakers or red flags. Since you are trying to avoid drama and heartbreak in your life, you have to listen to your friend, double checking the people you are attracted to against your initial list of desired qualities. This friend needs to be given the green light to call you out when you want to contact someone just because they are attractive, not because they meet your criteria list. When a person appears to meet your standards and your friend agrees, this is when you have to face your fears in order to take that next step by arranging a meeting.

The meeting should be intentionally limited time-wise, with lunch time during a work week usually a good option. For this reason dinner after work or meeting for a drink at a bar are not the best ideas. You want the meeting to end at a certain time. This ensures your safety, provides both of you a glimpse into the other and allows you to break away. Breaking away provides time for reflection on the date so you can make a sensible decision about going forward. Also, it provides a comfortable exit so that you are not wasting anyone's time if you realize you don't want to go any further in the relationship with this person.

The reality is you will meet many more people that will be wrong before you meet someone who may be right, unless you have screened very carefully and both you and your friend are great screeners. We already know that your screening ability is a bit imperfect, so hopefully your trusted friend is more objective. While the reality of this process is often frustrating, please keep in mind your goal. It is worth the inconvenience because when this process is completed, hopefully, you will never need to go through this again.

It's a lot like a job interview, and you have to go through this to find the best job you can find. Remind yourself: You are avoiding drama, heartbreak, wasted time and money - so it is worth it! Nothing wonderful is easily obtained. You don't find hundred dollar bills lying on the street when you are broke. When you need money, you have to find paying work. If you want a partner, you need to put in the effort.

When the meeting is arranged make sure someone you trust knows where you are and when you will be reachable for a follow up call after the date. Alcohol should be avoided, as well as bars, where it is too loud to comfortably talk. If the person you are getting together with is someone you know from your community, a few less precautions might be ok, but always keep the first meeting as a friendly get together in a public place.

It is possible, when you get a chance to know this person better, they will not be someone you want to get romantically involved with, so it isn't necessary to declare your intentions when you ask an acquaintance to go out to a movie or concert. By staying in public places until you are sure you want the relationship to go further you have a much greater ability to ensure the other person doesn't take things further than you are willing to go. Don't get in the person's car, or let them get you alone in your car, early in the relationship.

If your instincts are giving you a danger signal IMMEDIATELY GET YOURSELF OUT OF THE SITUATION HOWEVER YOU CAN. I had a client who was in an abusive relationship, but she was afraid to leave because her husband threatened she would never get custody of their child. This is a common threat, and a very effective one, especially when the woman isn't working and is without the necessary skills or degree to support herself.

This woman really wanted to move away to where her support system was in another state, but she knew that if she tried to move, he would never allow her to take her son. I asked, "what would happen if you went for a visit to see her parents", and then "things just kept happening", and eventually she never returned? She had to think this through for a while, eventually did exactly as I suggested, and a year later I got a letter from her thanking me for this advice. She couldn't believe how happy she was in her new life. Sometimes we just have to find ways to be creative.

Often I have counseled people who were abused as children or even as adults, invariably, they carry the fear of abuse into the next relationship. Many people who have experienced this type of trauma in their lives have difficulty trusting others or someone new. The unpredictability of a new relationship and a new situation is frightening. When your fear response is interfering with doing something new that would benefit you, I encourage my clients to write down their feelings in three steps:

1. Analyze your reaction and ask yourself is it based on fight, flight or freeze?

2. Ask yourself what it is you are afraid of?

3. Ask yourself what you need to feel safe, then relate the issue to this new person or figure out how you can create this safety on your own.

Let's apply this solution to a few sample scenarios based on my work with clients.

Case One: Wendy ended an abusive marriage three years ago. Now she is living with a boyfriend who is calm, thoughtful and supportive. Due to her past situation, Wendy has an exaggerated fear response wherein she expects something to change and go wrong. So, when feeling anxious she begins observing Jim extra carefully, watching for signs of his betrayal. If he talks about a female co-worker, she gets jealous and questions his interest/involvement with her. If they go somewhere public and he glances at another woman, she becomes accusatory and angry. Which in turn elicits an angry response from him over her distrust of him, causing him to withdraw. This further increases her fear of losing him.

If she applies the approach described above she will determine that her response to the fear is fight. What she is afraid of is losing his love and attention, and it makes her want to confront and fight with him.

His response is flight. If she continues to act this way it will cause him to withdraw more and more.

What does she need to feel safe? Wendy needs to believe that Jim has no romantic interest in this co-worker or that woman on the street. What can she do instead when she feels afraid? Wendy can reach for his hand, or in a calm and relaxed manner, Wendy can ask Jim to tell her what his favorite feature of hers is, or something he likes about her, or just ask Jim to tell her he loves her because hearing that would make her feel happy.

Note here the trick is to actively engage in both RECOGNIZING and SOLVING YOUR FEAR ISSUES. YOU have to actively ask your partner to support you in ways that will allow for these feelings of fear to dissipate over time.

Case two: Judy has recently married George and has a history of abandonment from her father. When they have their first few arguments, George likes to leave the home and go for a walk to calm down before discussing their disagreement. When George leaves, saying "I'm going for a walk", Judy freezes in terror. She shakes and feels she can't move or speak. Her breathing becomes restricted until he returns and her stomach is in knots the whole time. She takes a sedative to calm down, and by the time George comes home she is sleeping.

The next morning she wakes up after he has already left for work. She begins texting him urgently, thinking that he is leaving her for good, both attacking him and asking for reassurance, and her texts are so irrational he doesn't answer right away. She is terrified he is leaving and wants to end the relationship. Now she is in fight mode.

Judy wants to fight with him because she thinks he won't talk with her, thus he is abandoning her. Her irrational behavior prolongs the argument and their problem, when in fact all she really wants to know is he has no intention of leaving when he goes out for a walk.

If she can recognize she is freezing and try to take deep breaths, calming herself, she can try to talk with George before he leaves. She can ask where he is going and how long he will be gone. If he has already left, she has to wait for him to return and ask him why he leaves for a walk when they argue. She needs to relax her anxiety and find out why he reacts the way he does, not just focus on her feelings about his reactions.

Maybe he had a dysfunctional home where arguing was the norm and it makes him feel uncomfortable. Together, if they talk things out, they may be able to figure out how he can leave but reassure her that they will talk upon his return, but that he just needs some time and space to calm down first. Maybe he can leave his keys or wallet behind to reassure her when he leaves that he will return.

The important thing for Judy to do here is identify why his actions cause her to react in a certain way, figure out what type of reaction manifests itself when he does what he does and identify to him how she needs to have him behave so she can feel more at ease. They can discuss this, so the next time they argue, Judy won't go into such an intolerable fear state.

Case three: Henry is in a relationship with Cathy, who has just moved into his home. Henry is overly sensitive to criticism because his mother was very mean and cruel when she got drunk, which happened often while he was growing up. He has totally avoided alcohol all his life, keeping none in his home. Henry gets very tense and irritable every time Cathy buys a bottle of wine or opens it to have an evening glass. In addition, when Cathy asks to move something to make room for her belongings, Henry gets agitated, asking her if she doesn't like his taste in decorating.

Henry's response is to fight!

Cathy doesn't really understand the changes in his behavior, nor his constant irritation towards her, and wonders if she made a mistake moving in. This causes her to start withdrawing, which results in more irritable behavior from Henry. Henry talks to his therapist and realizes he is responding to his fears with a fight response. He is afraid of being criticized, judged and abandoned! He asks for a sit down with Cathy to figure out just how much space she will need. He asks her to share with him the decorating ideas she has for one of the rooms, so he can give her ideas some time to sink in and see if he likes them, or at least can live with them.

Henry does this because he realizes it is important for her to feel she has some input into their shared space. He asks Cathy how she feels about giving up her evening wine for a bit while he adjusts to the reality that alcohol does not bring out the worst in everyone. Because Henry calmly explains his reasons she feels much better about their new arrangement and is very willing to cut back her drinking habits until they are both more comfortable.

Henry has to realize his fight response to stress will cause their relationship to end if he continues his behavior, and he needs to learn how to cope with and control his response to fear.

The majority of conflicts between people occur because of our reactions to others and our interpretations of their behavior. Professional and personal experience has shown our reactions often have nothing to do with what is happening in the present time. More often than not, we are reacting to something else going on internally. IF WE DON'T IDENTIFY WHAT WE ARE FEELING AND WHAT WE NEED TO FEEL SAFE, OUR BEHAVIOR RESULTS IN RELATIONSHIP ISSUES BETWEEN OTHERS AND OURSELVES. Our most intimate partnership needs to be one based on honesty and trust.

We need to be honest with ourselves and our closest loved ones about what we're really afraid of and what we need. It is surprising how simple it can be to ask for what you need from others, even more amazing when that's all it takes for behavior and relationships to change. Give it a try, you may be in for a pleasant treat when your partner actually understands what is happening inside you and makes an effort to accommodate your requests to ensure you are happy.

Visualization for Courage:

Imagine yourself in a warrior stance, dressed in warrior ornaments. Imagine you are in this protective coating and standing on top of a mountain. Visualize your confident demeanor, your body is coursing with adrenaline - you are the manifestation of strength and fearlessness. Know that with your strength and courage, you can handle anything! How does this make you feel?

Alternative: Imagine yourself getting buckled into a specially outfitted racecar that has sides made of reinforced steel and airbags everywhere. You are in a racecar and the race is getting ready to start. You hear the gun signaling the start of the race, and you speed out into the pack of other cars. Imagine yourself hugging the curves of the road as you continue to feel confident and strong; passing others until finally you are in the lead and easily win the race.

Affirmation for Strength:

"I am strong, smart and confident. I have conquered many things in my life. I can handle anything life throws my way. I believe in myself."

five

Why You Do It; Are You "Addicted" to "Dope"?

I don't think it's a coincidence that people describe feelings of "being out of control" when they're stuck in an unhealthy relationship. Sometimes, even when they've ended the relationship, they continue to obsess about the other person for a long time after, which opens them up to repeatedly giving the person or relationship an additional chance. The feeling they are experiencing when they end this kind of relationship is very much like withdrawal, with the first day being the hardest and subsequent days slightly less hard.

My professional experience with crises interventions suggests most of the time the initial six weeks after a crisis is the most difficult period. The old adage about it taking 6 weeks to form a new habit or break an old one is true. If you can make it through 6-8 weeks without contact, generally you are on your way to moving forward with your life – and with healing! However, frequently there are incidental contacts along the way that can continue to trigger the whole cycle of feelings all over again. This process can indeed feel very physical and leave you feeling "out of control". Yes, as a professional, I have seen break-ups produce the same physical effects on a person as happens during withdrawals from drugs. Crazy huh?

Why is this happening? Why do otherwise smart people behave in such foolish ways when it comes to love? There could be a biochemical reason that people in these situations behave the way they do, and find it sooooo hard to change. It is possible the brain is responding as if there is an addiction, and that this process creates the feeling and behaviors of other addictions. If this is happening to you, or has happened, you are not alone.

Lets discuss the addicted brain and the processes that go on in it for a moment. Addictive behavior typically is activated in the nucleus accumbens area of the brain. In this area, chemical neurotransmitters activate the reward system that is involved in addiction and addictive behavior development. When this area of the brain is activated, there is a flood of the neurotransmitter called dopamine that is released, and we experience this flooding as pleasure.

Dopamine appears to be the primary pleasure biochemical. Many pleasurable things can trigger the release of dopamine, such as finishing a project or achieving an accomplishment. The way we feel when dopamine is released is similar to that of the high that occurs when first using certain drugs, drinking alcohol, completing a marathon or falling in love. Illicit drugs stimulate even higher releases of dopamine than normal daily experiences. Once people have experienced the "high" of the excessive dopamine release, they may continue to seek it out.

Over time, the same amount of stimulation no longer provides that same extreme response because the brain area begins to adapt or even maladapt. The amount of stimulation required to attain the same response increases which can create dependence and withdrawal when the stimulation is withdrawn. While the degree of stimulation is different between the brain's natural highs and those resulting from various drugs, it is possible to see the processes of adaptation and maladaptation are similar, and how we can indeed experience feelings akin to addiction in a relationship.

The power of that intense flooding is so pleasurable that we continue to seek it out, even when the source is no longer providing pleasure but pain. Our brains remember this rush of happiness and continue to seek experiencing it again.

Upon first meeting a love interest, the excitement we feel is that natural high of excessive dopamine being released. What a wonderful exciting feeling! When the relationship goes south, we can't quite believe that this wonderful "drug" isn't giving us the same high as it did before. Sometimes, we can keep going to that same source where we first felt that "high", even though it doesn't last and we end up feeling miserable. We keep trying again and again to have that same feeling, and the longer we do that, the harder it becomes to let go. Every now and then there seems to be a glimmer of hope that the person can change or care for us the way we need them to. It's a hard thing to let go of that fantasy which we tie to that feeling we first experienced. The drive to feel that rush of feelings again can propel us to act in some very foolish ways.

When reward and response behavior was initially being studied in the early 1900s, it was discovered that intermittent rewards built stronger conditioned responses. That is, with Pavlov's dogs, an initial response was 'trained' by giving dogs food at the same time a bell was rung. Later, when the bell was rung, the dogs still salivated. This was known as the 'trained/conditioned response'. The conditioned response was actually stronger and lasted longer if the reward was given sometimes rather than every time. In terms of time, the 'trained response' of salivation in the dogs would persist longer if the bell ringing was only sometimes paired with the reward of food.

In that same way, if the person you are involved with only occasionally rewards you with the attention you are seeking, it becomes harder for you to break the connection of expectation.

These two biochemical processes, dopamine flooding and conditioning, may be why it can seem so challenging to end an unhealthy relationship. Further, they may explain why we continue to seek out the same experience over and over, even when we already know the situation will have an unhappy ending. It's not just you being weak! It feels like an addiction and what is happening in your brain is possibly very similar to what an addict experiences. Like an addict you may have to take one day at a time without acting on the craving until your brain chemistry normalizes again.

In addicts, the recovery of the brain can easily take a year to break that cycle. REMEMBER that as you go thru the process of breaking your 'relationship addiction' RECOVERY TAKES TIME! Expect things to get much easier after the first six weeks. And fight with all your might to refrain from going back to the relationship or you will have to start the whole 'withdrawal process' over again.

Jasmine was a young woman I worked with who got involved with a narcissistic partner named Joey. Joey consistently put Jasmine down and criticized her. At some point, the compulsion to right things after they had gone wrong could cause her to call him hundreds of times in a day. Even a year later after they had no contact, the slightest event could remind her of Joey and trigger obsessive thoughts about him. The brain remembers the dopamine release and continues to motivate us to seek to feel that release again.

It's powerful, and it can be destructive or cause us to behave in self-destructive ways. We remember the flooding, the happiness, much more than the sadness and hurt. This mechanism is intended to steer us towards behaviors/sources that make us happy, help us survive and develop contentment, but it can go awry. The solution is to avoid the source of that stimulation, and identify alternative sources of happiness.

For this reason one of the best ways to get over an unhealthy relationship is to develop a new interest, hobby or exercise. In the meantime and at minimum, your daily processes will have to change to help you avoid the triggers reminding your brain of that flooding sensation you seek to re-experience. Being on an antidepressant during this time can help increase emission of some of the neurotransmitters to make this "withdrawal" easier.

Visualization for Breaking a Bad Habit:

Imagine that you are sitting in a customized chair made specifically for your body. The chair has exactly the right amount of support, cushion and padding to feel perfectly comfortable. The arms of the chair wrap around you, leaving you feeling very calm and safe. Pay attention to how relaxed you feel; how even and deep your breathing is when you are relaxed. Now imagine someone brings the object you are trying to resist into the room. They parade around the room with your 'coveted object' in hand.

Throughout this process you continue to pay attention to how calm you feel, how in control you feel and how the object in the room doesn't distract you or upset you at all. You begin to see the 'coveted object' doesn't compare to how you feel right now, thus it no longer draws you.

Affirmation for Self-Control:

"I have the power to control my decisions and my behavior. The more I control my behavior, the stronger and stronger I feel. I am proud of myself. I can do this."

six

Tips for Maintaining Happiness

Hopefully, you have followed the steps of this book and are now involved in a healthy, mutually respectful relationship. You might be wondering, since this is probably your first time in one, how do I endure it doesn't all unravel? I will be sharing with you some of the things I've learned from many years working with people, and perhaps the best use of this chapter is just review it, try the suggestions and see what works well for you.

I believe the most quoted maxim for happy relationships has been "never go to bed angry", but I don't agree. Sometimes, when we are in the middle of an argument we can't think straight. At times it may be best to let the dust settle, leaving things alone for a while. Drop it, let it go for now and make yourself a note on the calendar to have a discussion. After a good night's rest, sometimes the conflict seems so petty we wonder how it escalated into such a big argument. If that happens, you can cross it off the calendar. I believe the most important thing in a relationship is to learn how to comfortably disagree and resolve conflicts together! Taking the time to learn how each partner processes, reacts and perceives what happens.

So my rules to help maintain a healthy relationship are:

Don't talk about a problem when you're really upset!

In fact, the best way to discuss a problem is when it isn't happening and you are both in a good mood. If it is something that needs to be addressed, pick a time when you are both relaxed and ask your partner if it's ok to discuss something that is important to you. Whatever the subject is if it happened once, it is very likely to happen again. If it never happens again, then it's not really worth an argument. With this in mind, it's ok to wait for that moment to happen again before you voice your feelings. Only this time calmly ask your partner if you could talk about something that is bothering you and if it's possible could he/she change the behavior/action that is upsetting you. You need to be ready to explain why whatever it is triggers a negative reaction in you and the reason you would like them to consider changing this behavior/action.

Let me give an example from my own relationship: doing the dishes. I work late a few days a week and I am a vegetarian. When I come home late from work the last thing I want to do is wash dishes stained with meat products. I have asked my husband not to leave those dishes in the sink many times, but he forgets. This leaves me to decide whether or not this is worth getting really upset over. Instead of focusing on what he did not do, I try and focus on what he does do when I work late, which is to take care of my dogs and many other household chores.

When I think about the positives, I realize it's just not worth the argument and I make the choice to let the dirty dishes issue go.

If you exist in a relationship where all you do is point out each other's flaws the relationship won't last very long. Most of the things that annoy us just aren't all that important when you get right down to it. If you give some space between your response and the discussion, most things won't be worth spoiling the good mood and fun you are having the rest of the time. The less time you spend focused on those annoyances, and the more you focus on the positive aspects of your partner, the happier both of you will be. We all make mistakes and nobody is perfect! Learn to live with some of your own quirks so your partner can relax and be himself/herself.

ALWAYS REMEMBER, YOU CAN CHOOSE TO LET IT GO TOO.

Fight Fair! Learn how to argue fairly.

When you have a disagreement and emotions are running high, it is very easy to lapse into poor communication, name-calling and accusations. If you want to discuss something with the goal of getting a resolution, the conversation should avoid generalizations such as "you always" or "you never". Keep the context in the present and own your feelings using "me" statements. Make sure you take the time to properly identify what is bothering/scaring you most and ask for what you need to feel better.

Examples of "me" statements:

John, I wanted to know if it would be okay for me to talk to you about something that has been bothering me. When we fight and you go out for a walk, I get really scared you won't be coming back. It is my fear but it is real and I need your help overcoming it. I was wondering if it would be okay for me to ask you when you think you might return? Or would you mind letting me know when you will return by saying something like "I'm going out for a walk to calm down and I'll be back in a little while."

It is more important to be happy than to be right.

A valuable lesson I learned from my second husband. Many times, an argument occurs and the reason for the argument gets lost in the midst of the disagreement, thus the whole situation dissolves into a 'who is right battle'. LEARN TO LET THAT GO, BECAUSE WHO IS RIGHT ISN'T ANYWHERE AS IMPORTANT AS GETTING ALONG WITH EACH OTHER. The argument over who is right is one about acknowledging that the other person is smarter or better than you are.

No one wins that argument, because insisting on being right belittles your partner. We all need our feelings acknowledged, and that's one of the reasons people argue about this so often. Instead, acknowledge the other persons' feelings or, even better, give up a "you're right". A few "you're right, it's my fault" mea culpa's go a long way toward maintaining peace. If you don't believe me, ask my husband.

Take care of your partner as much as possible.

I can try to rub my back and you can try to rub your back, but it is a lot easier and feels a lot better if I rub yours and you rub mine. When we are focused on making our partners happy, often they will respond by making us happy. This rule is only true in a healthy relationship, which is why a good relationship is always with someone who is as capable of taking care of you as you are of them.

When you have something serious to talk about, do it face to face!

Turn off the TV. Sometimes these conversations spontaneously happen, but quiet everything around you when they do and face your partner. The type of 'ugly' behavior we can all easily slip into when using phones, texting or from different sides of the room very rarely happens when we sit face to face with our partners. Watch for your fear responses and acknowledge them as they come up. Try to listen and acknowledge what your partner is sharing, making sure you understand what they are saying. Remember the formula for controlling reactions: acknowledge your fear, figure out how you would feel safe and ask for what you need.

Maintain your focus on the present situation.

Discussions often lapse into arguments of blame that go deeper and deeper into the past. Blaming might release some of your tension, but it doesn't resolve any issues. You can't fix what has happened or has already occurred. Your goal isn't to be right or better, but to get along and be happy together. The most difficult thing to do in a discussion is just listen without responding; especially when you feel scared, afraid or angry.

The most important thing my husband needs me to do when he's upset about something, even if he is as much to blame as I, is just to listen to what it is he's upset about. THE HARDEST PART AS A LISTENER IS TO REMAIN NUETRAL.

Our first reaction is usually one of defense, explaining why we did what we did, which caused the other side to be upset. Our first reaction should be to simply acknowledge that the person is upset. You don't need to explain or justify at the onset, just acknowledge the feelings your partner is experiencing, that you understand you upset them and you will try harder not to upset them that way again.

Validate your partner's feelings

The most important thing that happens with a good friendship, and with a good therapist for that matter, is that each person's feelings are validated. No matter how or what you are thinking/feeling, there is always a reason for it. Many times when we air our grievances, we just want to be acknowledged, heard and/or understood. Professional experience has shown me this need is very strong in everyone, and is even stronger for those who have been in relationships that did not provide these feelings of acceptance and reinforcement.

Most times when someone is upset, VALIDATING THEIR FEELINGS AND THEIR RIGHT TO HAVE THEM IS THE MOST POWERFUL GIFT YOU CAN GIVE TO SOMEONE. If, instead, you get defensive and explain why you did what you did, an argument ensues and nothing gets resolved. The power of listening without interjecting your response can be very challenging. Try to just listen. Validate your partner's feelings by repeating back what you understand, checking to see if your interpretation of their feelings is correct. Then share that you understand why they are feeling the way they do and promise to give the issue more thought.

This is one of the most powerful ways to end an argument. When we have been in failed relationships over and over, fear, in the form of defensiveness, can make it very hard to listen to what the other person has to say to us, when, indeed, listening is often all that is really needed to solve the problem. Also, we need to share with our partners the fact we need this same behavior manifested towards us too. So, explain this to your partner. Ask for what you need.

Start with the assumption that whatever your partner did to upset you, it was not done with the intention of hurting or upsetting you.

Again, it is imperative you take some deep breaths before reacting. If you are reading this book, it's because you already have trust issues in relationships. You have been let down by those closest to you in the past, and will likely jump to the conclusion that poor behavior indicates you are going down the same path again. Quickly, you may assume this person is just like every other bad partner you have picked before.

Hold on though, maybe they're not! You picked consciously and carefully this time! How can you expect them to know all the ways you have been let down? How could they know your past relationships have conditioned you to react negatively, maybe to the point of losing your cool? So take some deep breaths and try to relax before you react. Stop and perform one of the visualizations or affirmations about safety we have worked on to help you relax.

Professionally and personally, I have seen and felt the power of these techniques. To this day I do them regularly, always with positive effects. And remember, tears are not unusual. They are a natural way to release stress or fear.

Visualization: Safety in a Relationship

Imagine yourself as a baby, see your current face on a baby and imagine now that you are the mother holding this baby and you know exactly what this baby needs to hear to feel safe. Tell yourself, you are safe, you are loved and I will always protect you. Nurture you! Take care of you. Imagine what it feels like to be wrapped in this warm blanket of love and security, rocking yourself gently back and forth, continuing to repeat whatever you need to hear. Rock until your baby self is calm and serene. Now embrace and enjoy the feeling.

Affirmation for Relationships:

"I am good and I am loveable. People are drawn to me. My friends and family love me, and I am safe."

seven

How to know if you need professional help or medications

You picked up this book because you continue to have the same go nowhere relationships. The first step is to try the new approach we've just gone over and see what happens. Please remember all new behavior patterns require repetition and practice to attain success. If you are getting stuck at a specific step, I suggest reading the relevant chapter over again to figure out where the mistake is occurring. Ask your trusted friend to objectively look over your actions, matched against the plan here in the book, to see if he/she can help identify what you should consider doing differently. If you don't achieve complete success, but see progress in one area, that's wonderful. You're on the right track!

However, if you continue to pick the wrong people and feel you can't control what you do, then you probably need some counseling in order to help you get to the bottom of why you continue displaying the same behavior. A therapist will also help you build your self-esteem, develop better coping skills and address lingering issues that seem to hold you back in life.

Maybe you've broken up with your partner over and over again, but your fear of being alone forever keeps you from moving on, so the pattern continues ad infinitum. Maybe you've found a wonderful partner but feel sure you will do something to sabotage your success. Perhaps you've found the right partner but feel you can't trust that person. You keep waiting for something bad to happen to prove your hypothesis there are no good partners out there for you, thus dooming you to be alone forever.

With each of these examples the same behavior is manifesting itself. If something inside you is continuing to sabotage your own success and happiness, then it's a good idea to get therapy. If you feel helpless to change any of the circumstances in your life, it is time to get professional help. The right therapist for you can save your life!

Many people have been to "counseling" and felt it wasn't all that helpful to them. Therapy is not for everyone. Oftentimes it can be because there exists a wide variety of backgrounds, philosophies and training programs in the profession, leading to a plethora of ways to work with clients. Much like clothes or cars, one size does not fit all. It's important to know what you want out of therapy, and whether the counselor you choose is able to help you achieve this based on their treatment methodology. Look for a counselor who has experience in short, client-centered treatment. Like every other goal discussed in this book, it's important to know what your objective is and to discuss this in the first appointment with your therapist.

Your first appointment with a therapist should be much like a job interview. You want to find out if they can help you by asking about the kind of approach they use, or the techniques they feel are most effective. You should be the one setting the tone and goals of your meetings. In the counseling situation, YOU ARE THE EMPLOYER and they are the employee, hired by YOU to reach YOUR goal.

While situations from your past definitely affect what is happening with your feelings and behavior today, it is not absolutely necessary to dig into everything in your past to solve what is in your way today. I have seen many situations where delving into the past can cause a functioning person to regress and deteriorate. Some situations don't benefit from excessively delving into them. The only piece of the past that is necessary to acknowledge is the part which is blocking you today, and then finding out what you can do about that block. It is up to you if you want to spend time dealing with some of your past, or if you want to focus on the present.

Your therapy time is time you have purchased to focus on what you want to focus on, and it is important that you do just that with your time. You should work with a therapist who lets you decide how often you need to come and when to return. If you haven't done your homework or tried this approach with a therapist your results may be less productive than hoped for, leaving you feeling your time and money were wasted.

When you are setting up your first appointment, it can be helpful to talk to the office staff, describing what you're looking for and what you wish to accomplish. Since they are the ones setting up the appointment, they should have an idea if what you're looking for and the style of therapist they represent match up. By all means, asking friends about their experiences can sometimes be helpful, but keep in mind your friend's needs could be completely different from yours.

Going to therapy is not a passive experience. The therapist isn't going to do the work for you. Change requires hard work and commitment, often taking years to achieve success. In the same vein that people make comments about how they need to lose weight as they eat a cheese Danish, nothing will change in your life without you deciding to make the change, committing to that change and doing the work necessary to bring about the change you desire.

A good therapist knows when medications will help make your life better, and can send you to a good provider. Just as people are fearful of going to a therapist, people can be even more fearful about taking medications. There are many misconceptions of what medications can and can't do for someone. I explain to my patients that a good medication is one with very few side effects, along with helping you feel like a more complete version of yourself. Medications should never make you feel like a zombie or change you into another person. Medications should help you better manage your life or your condition.

Medications are not always cures for a condition. Mental health issues and illnesses are no different than medical issues and illnesses. Most of them are chronic, meaning you need to figure out how to manage them as well as you can because they will be a part of your life. Many mental health conditions are completely or partially biological. The idea that will-power can be used to overcome and live with these conditions is as irrational as telling a diabetic if they stop eating their condition will go away! Medications are not habit forming, and being on one doesn't mean you will have to be on it the rest of your life.

It is important to take care of your mental health, because trying to ignore it will result in an enormous list of physical problems and illnesses over time. If you already have physical illnesses, then mental health issues will make them more disruptive to your life. Stress causes your body to secrete hormones that diminish your immune system and cause you to be more susceptible to illnesses. Even without a biochemical imbalance, the chaos and trauma you have been exposed to in your early life can continue to affect your health and functioning if it isn't treated in some way. Some people are lucky enough to be born into healthy families, or lucky enough to be resilient to long term stress without it affecting their lives. Others are not, and day to day life feels more like effort than living. If you have very little enjoyment or happiness in your life, or you have lost those enjoyments you used to have, then medication is probably a good idea for you.

As with many problems in life, it is important to make sure you are working with the right expert for the situation. Different treatment providers may suggest different treatment methods based on their field of study. Let's use a simple example like when you hurt yourself. If you go to your medical doctor, you may be told to put some ice on the injury and rest. If you go to a surgeon, he/she might suggest an operation because that is what they do. If you go to a psychiatrist, you might get medications and therapy sessions.

This is why it is important to research the person you are thinking of working with. If you don't have the time to work on your issues, medications are usually faster in helping you feel better or more in control of your feelings and behavior. If you are unsure of what you need, a therapist or your primary doctor can be a good person to steer you in the right direction.

Discuss with your provider whether the treatment is short or long term, how successful their treatment methods have been and what side effects might occur. Once you've accepted the idea that medication could be helpful to you, you might first start treatment with your primary doctor or you may prefer to go to a specialist, a psychiatrist or a psychiatric nurse practitioner like myself. Be clear about what you are hoping the medication will do to help you and ask the provider if this is a realistic expectation. Explain to the provider how your symptoms are interfering with your relationships and daily activities. Be honest about your thoughts, fears and beliefs regarding medications.

A good medication, I tell patients, is like the padding a football player wears. You should still feel the impact of everything going on, but the pain won't be as severe as it was without it. Anxiety, happiness and sadness are still present, but not to the point where they are overwhelming. In the relationship with the person prescribing, again you are the employer and they are the employee. If the provider doesn't respond to your concerns, find a new provider who listens. Medications don't cure most conditions; however, they do help to manage them. The best approach is often a combination of medication and therapy. Medication will help you feel better and cope better, but you still need to do the work to change your behavior. There are no magic pills that will change your life. The therapist will not do your work for you. Anything worthwhile is worth the effort, and changing or improving your life will require work on your part.

The good news, and I can attest to this fact after almost 35 years as a therapist, is people can and do change! LIFE DOES GET BETTER IF YOU WORK AT IT!

eight

My Favorite Books; Further Helpful Reading

In this chapter I share with you my favorite reading materials to help you continue on your journey to love and happiness. I've included the reasons I recommend them and what you can expect to gain from reading these books.

Each one has helped me on my journey to create a healthy and positive relationship in my life, filled with love and trust. The wisdom from these books for overcoming the behaviors that impede your happiness has been incorporated into my program laid out herein. You might want to read some of these more closely as they will enhance your understanding of the relevant issues affecting your life.

Clients who see me know that I buy certain books in bulk, which I have found to be particularly well-received and helpful for people on the path to fulfillment/happiness. There is nothing more disappointing than buying a book that seems to offer an answer to your questions, and then not find it there. I am constantly on the lookout for books that may be helpful to my clients. Here is a list of my favorite reading materials and authors.

A.) _Men Are From Mars, Women Are From Venus_ by John Gray PhD.

This book is one of the best books available explaining why women and men have so much trouble getting along. There are some absolute gems in this book! One of my favorites is about the different ways men and women respond to stress. For men, when they become aware of a problem, their goal is to fix it. For women, fixing the problem is not necessarily the goal. Often, women just want someone to listen to and validate their feelings regarding the issues and problems in their life. Men can find this 'venting without a goal of fixing the problem' very uncomfortable, as well as irrational.

When women talk about an issue, they feel it's most important to be heard, and often this is their main goal. Men find it hard to listen to a problem, and can feel very irritable/frustrated if it is a problem they can't fix. I always tell my clients "if you want something fixed, talk to a man, and if you just want to vent with someone to listen, do it with a woman." That being said, a healthy relationship happens when each side takes some steps towards the middle in order to live together in harmony.

B.) _Feel the Fear and Do it Anyway_ by Susan Jeffers PhD.

This book was given to me by my girlfriend as I was embarking on a new relationship with the man who eventually became my current husband. I knew I was dating a healthy man with the capacity to improve the quality of my life and, in doing so, give me a chance to break the cycle of abusive relationships I had always chosen. This scared me! I was terrified of allowing true intimacy into my life. Furthermore, I was just as terrified of sabotaging the relationship before this actually happened. _Feel the Fear and Do it Anyway_ gave me the tools to control my impulses so that I didn't act on them.

This book is very helpful for understanding the reality and commonality of fear, but more importantly, there is a very specific method for overcoming it. I used _Feel the Fear and Do it Anyway_ regularly; realizing the development of new skills would require help and a lot of practice in order to attain success. I used the method laid out, writing daily notes which included the steps and affirmations necessary to calm myself down. I kept the notes handy in my purse, on my computer and in my desk drawers. By reading the notes and regularly updating them, targeting what I was dealing with at the time, the book helped me control my behavior. As a result I was able to cope with overwhelming fear so that I could control myself and avoid sabotaging the relationship.

C.) _You Can Heal Your Life_ by Louise Hays

This book was given to me by my sister when I was going through a divorce. What I loved about it was that it restored a sense of hope for my future. This book introduced to me the practice of using affirmations and visualizations as a means of developing a positive mental outlook. Upon reading the book and seeing how effective the techniques were in my own life, I then incorporated much of the process into my professional practice. The ideas presented are grounded on CBT principles, essentially ones introduced in _Feeling Good the New Mood Therapy_ by Dr. David Burns, but this book offers them in a touchy-feely way, which can be more appealing to some people than the scientific approach offered in _Feeling Good the New Mood Therapy_. The practice of using affirmations and visualizations has been priceless to me in my personal life for helping deal with issues that felt insurmountable at the time. I have also attended programs by Louise Hays and found her to be very inspirational.

D.) _Feeling Good the New Mood Therapy_ by Dr David Burns MD.

One of two books that drastically changed my life, I read this book in college while I was getting my undergraduate degree in psychology at Loyola University in Chicago. I probably had been depressed since I was

14, and in therapy since I was 15. _Feeling Good the New Mood Therapy_ taught me how I could literally change my thinking with the result being significantly more control of my depression symptoms. I began writing down my thoughts whenever I was overwhelmed or upset, and when I felt ready, I would read them so I could figure out how my thoughts were contributing to my distrust, anger and sadness.

Since we usually repeat the same behaviors many times, I had ample opportunities at trying new approaches to confront my unhealthy thinking which, over time and through practice, allowed me to replace those harmful thoughts with helpful and productive ones. This book remains a gem, and an important one in my professional practice.

E.) _Getting the Love you Want_ by Harville Hendrix PhD

I read this book prior to my second marriage and found it very helpful. Essentially, _Getting the Love you Want_ explores the typical conflicts in relationships and their sources, in addition to offering exercises for resolving them. The author wrote this book at the end of a first marriage, before embarking on a second marriage that has proved to be successful. I remember doing the exercises to encourage openness and emotional intimacy prior to re-marrying, finding them to be very helpful. Also, _Getting the Love you Want_ offers helpful exercises and techniques for couples participating in counseling, or for a couple interested in improving their relationship on their own.

F.) _Stop Signs_ by Lynn Fairweather MSW

This is a second choice covering the dynamics and characteristics of abusive relationships. It details how to escape these once you're in one, which can be very helpful. There is a chapter about testing your partner to be sure they aren't an abuser. It describes the stages of abuse to help you recognize what is happening to you. It helps you understand that change of behavior by the abuser is rare and the fantasy of people changing abusive behavior is usually just that.

G.) _The 7 Habits of Highly Effective People_ by Steven Covey

This book uses the cognitive tools to explore how people interact with others, how to own your own behavior and how to effect change in your life. What I think _The 7 Habits of Highly Effective People_ adds to that discussion is the quality of character building; specifically, living your personal life based on self-respect and respect for others. The book provides a number of exercises for developing empathy, fairness and mutual respect in personal and business relationships. Character appears to be a quality lacking in many people today for numerous reasons. This book explores personality traits, with exercises to develop positive, healthy characteristics and methods of treating others in a way that values them while maintaining your self-respect.

H.) _CoDependent No More_ by Melody Beattie

CoDependent No More introduced the concept of co-dependency. Co-dependency occurs when you are involved with someone in a very unequal relationship. Usually there is a big red flag, such as alcoholism, drug abuse or infidelity. Somehow you can't extricate yourself from the relationship. This book helps you understand the dynamics involved and why you might be continually attracted to that kind of person, and how to break the dependence so that you take care of yourself. By owning your own behavior and co-dependence you can learn how to be an independent adult in the relationship, thus preventing yourself from getting drawn into the same pathological and painful blame game in which no one wins. An excellent and timeless book, still very relevant today!

G.) *How to Spot A Dangerous Man Before You Get Involved* by Sandra L Brown, MD

I think this book is an excellent companion to keep you on track as you are following the process outlined in my book. Many of the potential partners in your life might be toxic, and *How to Spot A Dangerous Man Before You Get Involved* is excellent for keeping you on track by identifying the non-dangerous partners as well as the dangerous ones. Partners can be dangerous because they can suck the life out of you by not holding up their weight in the relationship. A partner like that can have you paying alimony to them in the end! They are just as dangerous as the mental and physical abusers. This book gives great lists of 'identifiers' to help you spot them.

H.) *The Ghosts that Come Between Us* by Bulbul Bahugana MD

This novel delicately addresses the journey of a young girl coming of age in India who is dealing with an overpowering father that is sexually abusing her. Written by a noted psychiatrist who specializes in sexual abuse, *The Ghosts that Come Between Us* is a composite of various issues typically confronted by victims and takes a first person journey from victimization to health. The book is beautifully written; by the end leaving you with the feeling you know the narrator personally and have gone through the process alongside her.

The protagonist deals with overwhelming anger and, surprisingly, an overwhelming desire to protect the parent who was absent. In the end, the protagonist realizes she has to be the one to parent herself in order to heal the hurts of both parents; the one who did the abuse and the one who ignored the abuse.

nine

The End and the Beginning

Our lives are always in the process of restarting. When something hasn't been working we need to make a change. Now here you are, at the beginning of the next phase of your life. From this point on, you are focused on loving and respecting yourself, along with finding yourself a partner who supports mutual respect and values what you do in your life.

If you have followed the steps in this book, you now have a much clearer idea of what a healthy relationship looks like and you are keeping this idea FRONT AND CENTER in your mind as you go through your normal life activities. Remembering to stay alert to these ideas wherever you are, no matter what you are doing. On a regular basis, you should be taking a quick mental survey of your surroundings and opportunities to check if this could be a place you might meet the right person. Or evaluate a casual acquaintance to see if they are available and might fit your criteria.

REVIEW THE LISTS YOU HAVE CREATED TO KEEP YOU ON TRACK!

Every social opportunity or contact could lead to a possible connection in your life. Every day is another chance this could happen. Every place you go can be an opportunity to meet someone. Break your usual routines, expose yourself to more potential social opportunities and try new things. Keep in mind at all times what you're looking for.

The 'right people' to meet might be the ones you didn't notice before. They may be quiet and sometimes they are even those who have given up, yet deep down still have a lot to offer. I can't tell you how many lovable, wonderful people I see regularly in my practice who have just given up on the idea of having someone with which to share their lives. Sometimes I wish I could just introduce them!

Life is difficult and rejection can beat us down. I know that these people seem uninterested in meeting someone if you passed them in your daily travels, and you might assume they are already in a relationship or aren't interested in you – and you could very well be wrong! They might simply be a damaged bird that with a little love and care, could take flight again

You have bought and read this book because you're ready for something new and different. I have some good news for you. As I mentioned in the dedication, something seems to happen to people who read this book. I have yet to experience a single available person who upon reading this book, and enacting some of the ideas espoused, I didn't see sometime afterwards looking distinctly different, happier or tell me they were seeing someone.

I believe this has a lot to do with clarifying your goals and seeking to accomplish them, restoring your hope and belief that your future doesn't have to be unhappy, frustrating or lonely. When I have treated people with medications who are depressed about losing jobs, or financial hard times, it is not unusual that once their mood is improved, they get the next job they seek. Happiness and hopefulness are attractive qualities and make for good partners and employees.

If you take these steps to clarify what you're looking for in a partner and then make the room for someone to become part of your life, YOUR LIFE WILL CHANGE FROM HOW IT IS NOW. As you rid your life of people who waste your time, your love, your money and your energy - you will feel better. Your newfound confidence will help you both attract and keep people in your life who are worthy of your time and love. Emphasizing positive thinking and learning to love yourself will bring more happiness into your life in a variety of ways. It is my sincere hope that this book will help you accomplish all your dreams.

Acknowledgements

I would like to start off with thanking my wonderful husband Richie, my children, family, friends and close colleagues for their love and support through this treacherous journey we call life. It is indeed challenging and, because of all of your help, it has become very full and happy. Thank you for your patience through the process of this book becoming a reality.

Thank you to my friend, fellow yogi and co-writer and copywriter Stanley Crossland II. You took my words and ideas and turned them into prose. You held my hand through the process of rough draft through publication, spending countless hours helping me with your fantastic writing skills. I couldn't have done it without you, and I would never write another book with out begging you to co-author again with me. Thank you for your support, skills, talent and artistic vision. The day our lives crossed paths was indeed fortuitous for me.

Thank you to Dr Bulbul Bahugana and the Lilly sales representative, Cara Stader, who led me to her, and Dr Dawn Levitan. You gals were my beacons!

www.ingramcontent.com/pod-product-compliance
Lightning Source LLC
Chambersburg PA
CBHW071050290526
45795CB00004B/1424